DATE DUE

APR 1 7			
GAYLORD			PRINTED IN U.S.A.

Miranda v. Arizona

Rights of the Accused

Gail Blasser Riley

Landmark Supreme Court Cases

Enslow Publishers, Inc.

40 Industrial Road	PO Box 38
Box 398	Aldershot
Berkeley Heights, NJ 07922	Hants GU12 6BP
USA	UK

http://www.enslow.com

This book is dedicated with love and respect to my family:
to my dad, Marvin, for teaching me to build castles in the air while
keeping my feet planted firmly on the ground;
to my husband, Jim, for believing in me and in this book;
to my children, Rachel, Jillian, and James, for being the best of me
and for inspiring me to be my best.

Library of Congress Cataloging-in-Publication Data

Riley, Gail Blasser
    Miranda v. Arizona: rights of the accused / Gail Blasser Riley.
      p. cm.
    Includes bibliographical references and index.
    ISBN 0-89490-504-X
    1. Miranda, Ernesto — Trials, litigation, etc. — Juvenile
literature. 2. Trials (Rape) — Arizona — Juvenile literature.
3. Self-incrimination — United States — Juvenile literature.
4. Right to counsel — United States — Juvenile literature.
5. Police questioning — United States — Juvenile literature.
[1. Police questioning. 2. Miranda, Ernesto — Trials,
litigation, etc. 3. Civil rights — History.] I. Title.
II. Title: Miranda versus Arizona.
KF224.M54R55 1994
345.73'056 — dc20   93-34380
[347.30556]   CIP
                                                  AC

Printed in the United States of America.

10 9 8 7

Photo Credits: Ackad, Collection of the Supreme Court of the United States, p.
96; © *Arizona Republic*, February 1, 1976; Used with permission. Permission does
not imply endorsement, p. 93; Courtesy of the Library of Congress, pp. 18, 24;
Courtesy of Peter Baird, Attorney at Law, p. 91; Franz Jantzen, Collection of the
Supreme Court of the United States, p. 74; RG107, Maricopa County, SG 8,
Superior Court 1963-1971. Phoenix, AZ: Arizona State Archives, Department of
Library, Archives and Public Records, pp. 9, 12, 43; RG 107, Maricopa County,
SG2, Attorney, 1962–1975. Phoenix, AZ: Arizona State Archives, Department of
Library, Archives and Public Records, pp. 47, 62, 89.

Cover Photos: Franz Jantzen, "Collection of the Supreme Court of the United
States" (background); Harlee Little (insert).

Contents

Acknowledgments:

The author would like to offer special thanks to:

James M. Riley, Jr., Esq., for extensive assistance and legal expertise in preparation of this mansuscript.

Babs Bell Hajdusiewicz for tireless aid, friendship, and levity in preparation of this manuscript.

Kristine C. Woldy, Esq., for friendship, candor, and legal expertise in preparation of this manuscript.

Laurie Lazzaro Knowlton for insisting on "this whole writing thing."

Sally Lee, for getting the ball rolling on this book.

Peter Baird, Esq., for information and inspiration.

Moise Berger, Esq., for personally taking me back to the second Ernesto Miranda trial.

David Hoober and Carolyn Grote, and the staff of the Arizona State Archives, for everlasting assistance and consideration.

Ray Tevis and staff, Arizona Department of Library, Archives and Public Records.

Bill Shover and Nancy Van Leeuwen, *Arizona Republic.*

Franz Jantzen, Supreme Court Curator's Office.

Barbara Natanson and George Hobart, Library of Congress, Prints and Photographs Division.

Bebe Overmiller, Mary Eisen, and staff, Library of Congress, Photo Duplication Division.

Chris MacGregor and staff, Imagination Plus, The Woodlands, Texas.

Mark Meader and staff, National Archives, Motion Picture Sound and Video Branch.

John Vandereet, National Archives, Civil Division.

Kathleen Schrader and staff, Phoenix, Arizona Police Department Records Division.

Melissa Thompson, Maricopa County Attorney's Office.

1

You Have the Right to Remain Silent

"You have the right to remain silent . . ."

The theater screen had been anything but silent on the night of March 2, 1963. Guns had blazed, and dying men had screamed. But *The Longest Day* had come to an end. Credits had rolled, and the movie theater in Phoenix, Arizona was quiet again.

Eighteen-year-old Rebecca Ann Johnson* finished her duties at the theater refreshment counter and took a few minutes to visit with a fellow worker. It was 11:30 P.M.

---

* In courtesy to the victim, her real name is not used.

when, as usual, Rebecca Ann left the Paramount Theater to head for the bus stop.[1]

She could not have known, however, as she boarded the bus, that her nightly routine was about to be shattered. On that March night in 1963, the life of Rebecca Ann Johnson would, in a matter of hours, be changed forever. She was on the verge of being drawn into one of the most controversial landmark cases in the history of the United States Supreme Court.

It was 12:10 in the dark morning hours when Rebecca Ann stepped off the bus and began her short walk home. As she walked, a car pulled sharply out of a driveway. Rebecca Ann jumped back to avoid being hit. The car pulled into the street, moved a short distance, and stopped.

Rebecca Ann was caught unaware when a man from the car approached and grabbed her around the waist. The assailant covered her mouth and warned, "Don't scream and I won't hurt you."[2]

On March 3, 1963, Ernesto Miranda kidnapped the terrified Rebecca Ann Johnson.

He forced her to lie down in the back seat of his car, bound her hands and feet with rope, and then drove to the Arizona desert, where he raped her.

Approximately two hours after he had grabbed her from a Phoenix street, Miranda returned Rebecca Ann to her neighborhood. Oddly, his parting words were, "Whether you tell your mother what has happened is none of my business, but pray for me."

Rebecca Ann ran from the car, too frightened to check the license plate number. She raced the few blocks home and, between sobs, spilled the details to her sister.[3]

Rebecca Ann's nightmare had begun. The man who had committed this horrifying crime against her was Ernesto Miranda, and he would carry Rebecca Ann's future into the courtroom and the headlines. His name was to become a verb in the English language as police, prosecutors, defense attorneys, and judges would speak of "Mirandizing" a suspect for decades to come.

Rebecca Ann detailed her terrifying night to police. She described her attacker and his automobile. Specifically, she told police that a long rope had been draped across the back of the front seat, perhaps for passengers to pull up on to get out of the car.[4]

During repeated interviews, Rebecca Ann's detailed statements were sometimes inconsistent. Her account of the route to and from the desert posed inaccuracies. Further problems arose when Rebecca Ann was subjected to a polygraph test. Officers began to doubt whether Rebecca Ann was telling the truth.[5]

On March 9, 1963, at approximately 11:45 P.M.,

On March 3, 1963, Ernesto Miranda forced Rebecca Ann Johnson into this car. Officers Cooley and Young found the Packard automobile in Miranda's driveway on March 13, 1963.

Rebecca Ann's brother-in-law was on his way to meet her at the bus stop. He saw a car matching the description of the attacker's automobile, noted the license plate number, and reported it to the police.

Detectives ran a check and found an almost identical license number. They traced the number to an address where they found the matching license plate on a Packard automobile parked in the driveway. Inside the car, officers found a rope draped across the back of the front seat. Ernesto Arturo Miranda was taken into custody.

At the police station on that same day, March 13, 1963, Rebecca Ann thought she recognized Miranda in a lineup. But she wasn't positive.

After the lineup, police took Miranda to an interrogation room, a room for questioning.

"How did I do?" Miranda asked.

"You flunked," answered one of the officers.[6]

This response was not accurate, as Rebecca Ann had not been able to make a positive identification. Nonetheless, the detectives began questioning Miranda, and he signed a confession approximately two hours later.

What would happen to Miranda's confession in court? Would he later deny his confession? Would Rebecca Ann Johnson be able to identify her attacker at

Ernesto Miranda, wearing number 1, was placed in a lineup at the Phoenix, Arizona police department on March 13, 1963.

the trial? How would a surprise witness help win a conviction? Why, out of thousands of kidnappings and rapes that had come before, would Ernesto Miranda's case be decided by the Supreme Court and affect every arrest in the United States from that day forward?

2

Steppingstones to Miranda's Court Challenge

On a Friday night in 1936, a deputy sheriff and two companions arrived at the home of Yank Ellington and demanded that he come with them. When the three arrived at the house of a murder victim, a mob began to shout accusations at Ellington. Ellington denied the accusations. The mob grabbed him, dragged him to a nearby tree, and hanged him by a rope to a limb of the tree. Still alive, Ellington, the accused, was let down. When asked to confess, he still denied having committed the crime. The mob hanged him again from the tree limb and whipped him as he dangled in the air.

When Ellington was let down the second time, his neck was burned from the ropes that had eaten into his flesh.

He continued to proclaim his innocence. The mob then tied him to a tree and whipped him. He still refused to confess. The mob finally released Ellington. In "intense pain and agony," he managed to return to his home.

Two days later, the deputy came to arrest Ellington. The two men took a long route to the police station, actually driving through another state. On the way, the deputy stopped and severely whipped Ellington, telling him that the whipping would continue until he agreed to confess. His will broken and his body in great pain, Ellington finally agreed to confess to the murder, and the deputy took him to the police station.

At the station, two other men accused as accomplices in the crime were forced to strip and were laid over chairs. Their backs were "cut to pieces with a leather strap with buckles on it," and they were threatened that the punishment would continue until they confessed. They were tortured until every detail of their confessions matched the details "desired by the mob."[1]

This is not an excerpt from a book of fiction. Rather, it is the account of facts, as they were described in the 1936 United States Supreme Court case of *Brown* v. *The State of Mississippi*.

United States legal history has taken many twists and turns in arriving at the present-day state of affairs, in which the rights of the accused are of extreme importance in law enforcement. In times past, confessions were routinely "beaten out of" suspects, and the right to an attorney for the accused in a criminal trial was not available in all situations. Ernesto Miranda's case occurred at the peak of decades of legal battles focusing on the rights of the accused.

Why was Ernesto Miranda's case so important? What were the legal steppingstones that led to the Supreme Court's decision? Why did this case so sharply divide opinions across the country?

In order to get a clear picture, we must travel across the ocean and back through time to the seventeenth century, when John Lilburne, a Puritan publisher in England, was charged with the crime of importing heretical and seditious books into his country. These were books that disagreed with popular views of that time and challenged the government's authority.

When ordered to the Star Chamber, known as the scene of forceful interrogation, Lilburne steadfastly refused " 'to take a legal oath' and 'answer truly.' " He was refusing to act as a witness against himself, an advantage Ernesto Miranda would not later choose at the police station. Lilburne was whisked away and whipped, fined, and imprisoned. Four years later, Lilburne was released when the English government declared his treatment illegal.[2]

Lilburne's famous case was one of the first stepping-stones in due process development. It was an integral part of the momentum which would catapult Ernesto Miranda's appeal to the United States Supreme Court.

Due process is a protection against arbitrary government proceedings. It guarantees that an individual shall be told of the charges made and that the individual shall be given the opportunity for personal defense. In addition, due process protection provides that action by a state must be consistent with the fundamental principles of liberty and justice.

In examining the legal history which led to Miranda's successful Supreme Court appeal, rights provided in three amendments within the Bill of Rights, the first ten amendments to the United States Constitution, are extremely important. These include the Fifth Amendment privilege against self-incrimination, the Sixth Amendment right to have an attorney at the time of a criminal trial, and the Fourteenth Amendment due process guarantee of fundamental fairness.

When analyzing the development of confession law in the United States, the Fourteenth Amendment must be carefully considered. In order to understand why, a grasp of the difference between federal and state court systems is essential.

Some crimes violate state statutes, which are laws

John Lilburne refused to act as a witness against himself.

written at the individual state level by the members of the House of Representatives and Senate. Violations of these laws occur within the state and are prosecuted first in the state trial courts. Examples of state criminal statutes include laws against murder, theft, rape, and kidnapping, when the victim is not taken across state lines.

Some crimes violate federal statutes, which are laws written at the federal level, in Washington, D.C., by members of Congress. Violations of these laws are prosecuted first in federal trial courts. Examples of federal statutes include laws against treason, federal income tax evasion, and kidnapping, when the victim is taken across state lines.

Of critical importance here is the fact that the Fifth Amendment privilege against self-incrimination and the Sixth Amendment right to an attorney at trial originally applied only to criminal cases in federal courts. Therefore, if a state law such as murder or theft had been violated, the Fifth and Sixth Amendments did not protect the accused.

If this had remained the state of affairs, Ernesto Miranda's case would likely never have made it to the United States Supreme Court in the 1960s. His Fifth Amendment rights would not have been an issue, as his kidnap and rape charges were violations of state statutes, not federal.

Over many decades, however, new steppingstones for Miranda's case would develop. Utilizing guarantees of fairness in the Fourteenth Amendment, the United States Supreme Court would one day apply Fifth and Sixth Amendment rights at the state level. This application would be based on the fact that fundamental fairness, a guarantee in the Fourteenth Amendment, required that the Fifth Amendment privilege against self-incrimination and the Sixth Amendment right to an attorney at a criminal trial be applied to state proceedings, as well as federal proceedings. The process used to apply the Fifth and Sixth Amendments to the states using the Fourteenth Amendment due process clause is known as the incorporation doctrine.

Long before the incorporation doctrine developed, the legal rules applied in John Lilburne's and later English cases became law in the United States by way of the Fifth Amendment to the United States Constitution. The Fifth Amendment states: ". . . No person . . . shall be compelled in any criminal case to be a witness against himself . . ."

Thus developed the famous line: "I plead the Fifth." Little was it known when this phrase was first used in courts across the country, and later in films, that its counter-part—"You have the right to remain silent . . ."— would become perhaps even more recognizable.

The Fifth Amendment provides that people cannot be forced to make incriminating statements about themselves in criminal trials. A defendant may choose to testify, give information on the witness stand about a case, or may choose not to testify. Failure to testify may not be used against the defendant, nor may it be considered for any purpose. Indeed, if the defendant does not testify, the prosecutor, the lawyer representing the state, and the victim may not even mention the defendant's failure to testify to the jury.

In 1931, the National Commission on Law Observance and Enforcement, also known as the Wickersham Commission, examined the brutality used in extracting confessions. "Commission investigators had documented hundreds of examples of beatings, pistol whippings, strappings, lynching threats, solitary confinement in rat-infested jail cells, application of the 'water cure'—holding a suspect's head under water for long periods—and protracted [very lengthy] questioning, all in an effort to elicit confessions for offenses that ranged from murder to stealing a hog."[3]

The commission's conclusion was: "It is not admissible to do a great right by doing a little wrong. . . . It is not sufficient to do justice by obtaining a proper result by irregular or improper means."[4] This report gave a whole new meaning to the phrase, "The end does not justify the means."

Before the Wickersham Report, the philosophy of the United States Supreme Court centered on a "hands-off" doctrine with respect to overturning state criminal court decisions. What was the reasoning behind this doctrine? Because the states were allowed to make their own laws, they should be permitted to handle the enforcement of those laws on their own, through their state courts, without the interference of the United States Supreme Court.

After the Wickersham Report, however, the Supreme Court's philosophy began to change. Shockingly evil cases came to the attention of the Justices. No longer would it seem appropriate to step back and exercise a "hands-off" posture. The Fourteenth Amendment to the Constitution guaranteed fairness to all Americans. Supreme Court Justices found that the Fourteenth Amendment due process rights were being violated; confessions were being extracted in unfair, unjust ways.

The Fourteenth Amendment, Section 1, states: ". . . nor shall any State deprive any person of life, liberty, or property, without due process of law . . ." This amendment requires fundamental fairness, meaning that cruel or arbitrary procedures must be avoided.

The Fourteenth Amendment has been of great

importance throughout legal history in the United States. As early as 1932, the case of *Powell* v. *Alabama* came before the United States Supreme Court. In that case, better known as the "Scottsboro Nine" case, nine minority males were charged with the murder and rape of two Caucasian girls. In the state court, the judge appointed all the lawyers in the courtroom to represent the nine defendants. All but two attorneys withdrew from the case. And the two remaining had no opportunity to investigate on behalf of their clients. The attorneys consulted with their clients for only thirty minutes before going to trial. Eight of the defendants were convicted and sentenced to death. The jury was unable to make a decision as to the ninth defendant.

The eight defendants who were convicted appealed. For the first time, the United States Supreme Court overturned a state criminal court conviction due to an unfair trial. The Court used the Fourteenth Amendment as the basis for its decision. Because the indigent defendants, those people unable to afford to hire an attorney for themselves, had not truly had the aid of attorneys who could help with their defense, the Court ruled that due process of law had been violated. The result was that the defendants had not been granted fundamental fairness; thus, their convictions were violations of the Fourteenth Amendment.[5]

Nine years after receiving a life sentence, Clarence Norris, one of the defendants convicted in the "Scottsboro Nine" case, leaves his prison cell in Montgomery, Alabama.

Had it not been for this steppingstone, had the Supreme Court not stepped in and ruled regarding a state court criminal trial, Ernesto Miranda's case could never have made it to the highest court in the land.

It is important to consider United States Supreme Court decisions such as *Powell* v. *Alabama* because each one sets a precedent. A precedent is a legal decision providing a rule of law which should be observed in future cases with the same or very similar facts. For this reason, Supreme Court decisions make a forceful impact on the future of our country.

Shortly after the *Powell* case, *Brown* v. *Mississippi*, discussed earlier, was decided by the United States Supreme Court in 1936. In the *Brown* case, police physically brutalized the suspects in order to force them to confess to murder. The three minority male suspects were subjected to beatings, whippings, and long periods of questioning where they were not allowed to talk to anyone other than police. It is no wonder that they confessed after such torture.

When their trial began and the defendants appeared in the courtroom, their wounds were clearly visible. And witnesses admitted having beaten the defendants. Even so, the confessions were accepted, and the defendants were sentenced to death by hanging.

The death sentence was not carried out because the

Supreme Court, shocked at the methods used to obtain the confessions, reversed the convictions. Just as it had in the *Powell* v. *Alabama* decision, the Court based its ruling on the Fourteenth Amendment, which was quite significant in cases of this type. The Court found that confessions obtained through beatings "violated the fundamental right to a fair trial," that "the rack and torture chamber may not be substituted for the witness stand." Still, the Supreme Court decision clearly stated that the self-incrimination clause of the Fifth Amendment did not apply to the states, that the decison in *Brown* v. *Mississippi* was based on the Fourteenth Amendment, not the Fifth Amendment.[6]

The *Brown* decision provided another steppingstone for Miranda. Although Miranda's situation certainly did not parallel Brown's, since Miranda's involved no beatings or whippings, Brown was in some ways a soul mate to Miranda. Brown's Supreme Court case began to pave the way for Miranda's Supreme Court challenge.

The *Brown* decision played a meaningful role in the legal history of the United States. Still, in the 1930s, at the time of the *Brown* opinion, the Fifth Amendment privilege against self-incrimination and the Sixth Amendment right to an attorney had not been applied to cases in state courts.

Although certain rights flowed to the accused through

the Fourteenth Amendment, this amendment alone did not provide strong enough constitutional protection. It failed to thoroughly protect the rights of the accused. Why did the Supreme Court ultimately decide to take further steps to guarantee the constitutional rights of the accused and apply the Fifth and Sixth Amendments to state court proceedings? A further examination of the *Brown* case and the cases that followed will help to answer this question.

Before the *Brown* case, the Supreme Court had generally not reviewed state cases which dealt with the admission of confessions into court. As a result, convictions at the state level generally became final.

Also, before the *Brown* opinion, the courts had been much more concerned with the veracity, that is the truth, of the confession than with the manner in which the confession had been obtained.

Given the atmosphere in the country and the impact of the Wickersham Report, the Supreme Court, in the *Brown* case, began to take a new look at laws governing confessions. From that time on, a new test would develop, one that Ernesto Miranda's confession would later pass in the state court.

This new test would become a due process balancing act of sorts. It would come to be known as the "voluntariness" or "totality of the circumstances" test. In determining whether a confession had passed the test, the court would weigh the factors that determine the suspect's ability to resist police coercion. Factors such as age, intellect, education, and prior experience with the police would be weighed against physical brutality, threats, withholding of food or sleep, and long periods of questioning.

This equation would result in a decision regarding the "voluntariness" of the confession. Using the balancing test, a judge would determine whether the confession was voluntary, that is, given without coercion. If so, the confession could be heard in court and considered when determining whether the defendant was to be found guilty. If found to be involuntary, the confession could not be heard in court. It could not be used to determine whether the defendant was to be found guilty.[7]

One Supreme Court Justice explained the reasoning behind the test by stating, "What would be overpowering to the weak of will . . . might be utterly ineffective against an experienced criminal."[8] The Justice's support for the voluntariness test was clear.

Other Supreme Court Justices, such as Justice Hugo L. Black and Justice William O. Douglas, both of whom would go on to champion Ernesto Miranda's cause, found this voluntariness balancing approach totally inappropriate. They believed that a case-by-case approach was vague and unfair. The trial courts were given too much freedom in determining how to apply the test under the Fourteenth Amendment.

How could it be that two suspects who were treated exactly the same by the police during questioning could have totally opposite outcomes regarding their confessions, the Justices considered.

What if different state court judges weighed the factors differently?[9]

Though confession law had evolved dramatically from the days when the Supreme Court generally did not even consider state confession cases, dissatisfaction with the law remained. It is true that the *Brown* case and many cases that followed were instrumental in protecting the rights of the accused and in forming the backbone of confession law in the United States. The "totality of the circumstances" test, however, failed to provide a uniform test to protect the constitutional rights of suspects accused of crimes. And still, the United States Supreme Court had yet to deal with many issues from the state level, issues such as the right to remain silent and the right of the accused to have an attorney after being taken into custody, prior to the time of the trial.

Then, in 1963, the United States Supreme Court opinion in the landmark case of *Gideon* v. *Wainwright* applied the Sixth Amendment, the right to counsel, to state criminal court proceedings. Before this case, not all defendants in state court trials had the right to be represented by an attorney. A state could write its own law granting the right to an attorney, but if it did not, this right generally did not exist (except in rare circumstances) because the Sixth Amendment applied only to proceedings in federal courts, not to those in state courts. Thus, in a state court criminal proceeding, if the defendant wanted a lawyer but was indigent, could not afford a lawyer, the judge was generally under no obligation to appoint an attorney to represent the accused.

The *Gideon* decision would change that. Clarence Earl Gideon was on trial for breaking and entering a pool room. He asked that the judge appoint an attorney to represent him, as he was indigent. The state court judge refused to appoint a lawyer, commenting that this was not the practice in the county.

Upon appeal, the Justices of the Supreme Court *made* it the practice and brought the United States one step closer to its opinion in the *Miranda* case. In a unanimous decision, the Court applied the Sixth Amendment, through the Fourteenth Amendment, to the states.[10] From that time forward, the law required that a lawyer be appointed to represent the indigent defendant charged with a felony, an offense punishable by a year or more in prison. In 1972, the United States Supreme Court would extend the indigent's right to counsel in *any* case where the defendant was sentenced to imprisonment, even if for one day.[11]

The *Gideon* opinion was a necessary steppingstone for Ernesto Miranda's case. Miranda's case dealt with the right to have an attorney during interrogation before the time of trial.

If the right to a lawyer at the time of the state criminal trial itself had not been created through the *Gideon* decision, it is highly unlikely that the right to a lawyer during interrogation, before the trial would ever have arisen.

During the 1960s, the decade of the *Gideon* decision, new and different concerns regarding confessions became evident. Even though some of the more brutal physical methods of questioning had diminished somewhat, other methods became popular. These underhanded tactics revolved around clever, sometimes less obvious psychological approaches.

A former district attorney recalled a particular station house interrogation scene from the 1960s. Officers were trying to get a suspect to make a statement. The officers told the suspect to remove his clothing. The suspect bravely removed his shirt, his pants, his shoes, his socks, but not his underwear. When officers told him to remove his underwear, he refused. Rather than strip bare, the suspect asked, "What do you want to know?"[12]

Though confessions gained from this type of questioning did not involve physical brutality, they imposed another type of pressure. The suspect's constitutional rights and the protection of these rights remained complex and critical issues.

In 1964, just after the *Gideon* decision, the Supreme Court handed down its opinion in the *Malloy* v. *Hogan* case, another significant break for Ernesto Miranda. In this case, Malloy had been called upon to testify in a state hearing regarding gambling and other crimes. Malloy was on probation for a gambling offense. During the state hearing, he refused to answer questions regarding his earlier arrest and conviction, asserting his Fifth Amendment privilege against self-incrimination. Malloy was held in contempt of court, ordered to prison, and told he would remain there until he agreed to answer.

The Supreme Court ruled that Malloy's constitutional rights had been violated. In making their decision, through use of the incorporation doctrine, the Justices utilized the Fourteenth Amendment to apply the Fifth Amendment privilege against self-incrimination to state court proceedings. No longer would the Fifth Amendment privilege against self-incrimination be denied to defendants in state courts.[13]

The *Malloy* case was a huge steppingstone for Ernesto Miranda. Still, all the necessary Supreme Court decisions were not yet in place to lead to the future reversal of Miranda's state court conviction. Important issues, such as the right to an attorney during interrogation and the right to remain silent after arrest, had yet to be ruled upon in a light favorable to Miranda.

A breakthrough for Ernesto Miranda and a man by the name of "Danny Escobedo" came shortly after the *Gideon* and *Malloy* decisions. If Brown and Miranda were unwitting soul mates, then surely Escobedo and Miranda were unwitting "brothers in history."

Danny Escobedo was living in Chicago in 1960. In the early hours of a cold winter morning, he was picked up by police officers and taken in for questioning. Escobedo's brother-in-law had been murdered several hours earlier. Escobedo made no statement and, through his attorney's efforts, was released.

Ten days later, Escobedo was again arrested, this time with his sister-in-law, the victim's widow. In the car, on the way to the police station, officers gave Escobedo a piece of startling news. Escobedo should confess, they advised, because his good friend, Benedict DiGerlando, had already told them the "truth," that Escobedo had fired the fatal shots.

Keeping his wits, Escobedo did not offer a statement,

but asked for his lawyer. Escobedo's lawyer arrived at the police station and saw his client through the occasionally-opened door of the interrogation room. At one point, the two even waved to each other. Still, repeated requests by Escobedo and his attorney to confer were denied. Finally, the lawyer left to file a complaint with the Chicago Police Commissioner.

A short time later, DiGerlando was brought into the interrogation room by police. Escobedo shouted, "I didn't shoot Manuel. You did it!"

The police finally obtained a signed confession from Escobedo. He admitted having paid DiGerlando $500 to commit the murder.

At the trial in state court, Escobedo denied his confession. He said that he had been tricked into making it, and that the police had promised he would be released and would not be prosecuted if he would just sign the confession form.

The confession was not thrown out. Escobedo was sentenced to life in prison. He appealed his conviction. When his appeal reached the United States Supreme Court, his conviction was reversed. The Court's opinion stated that Escobedo should have been granted the right to speak to his attorney upon request, that he had been denied his constitutional rights under the Sixth and Fourteenth Amendments.[14]

Little did Danny Escobedo know when he was arrested on a bitterly cold morning in January of 1960 that his case would ignite so much controversy in the Supreme Court of the United States. And little did Ernesto Miranda know on that January morning that a man in Illinois was about to pave the way for a Supreme Court decision that would make Miranda famous.

Escobedo's and Miranda's names would become linked for all time in fame or infamy, depending upon which side of the political climate future critics supported. Though no warning cards (cards carried by police officers to advise arrested suspects of their rights) would come of Escobedo's Supreme Court challenge, his name, and his case, would become almost as famous as Miranda's.

In ruling on Escobedo's appeal, the Supreme Court utilized the Fourteenth Amendment to apply the Sixth Amendment right to counsel, just as the Court had done in the *Gideon* case. In the *Escobedo* decision, however, the Supreme Court went one step further than it had in the *Gideon* opinion. The Court ruled that the suspect had the right to have a requested attorney present prior to the time of trial, during questioning.

In the 1960s, the time of the *Gideon* and *Escobedo* decisions, the Supreme Court was often referred to as the "Warren Court," since its Chief Justice then was Earl

Warren. So-called "liberals," who strongly supported the civil rights of the individual, supported the Supreme Court with equal force.

A division had been forming in the country, however. Some Americans felt that the Supreme Court was falling off of its tightrope in the balancing act of protecting individual rights versus protecting society's or victims' rights.

The Court had upheld civil rights by declaring segregation in schools unconstitutional. Further, the Court had disturbed local political practices by ordering changes regarding voting districts. These decisions angered some Americans.[15]

And many Americans were furious with the decisions of the Court regarding the rights of the accused. Decisions such as *Powell, Brown, Gideon,* and *Malloy* were particular sore spots for these critics. And they became even more distressed when the *Escobedo* decision was handed down.

The *Escobedo* decision set off waves of anger and fear through various segments of the American public. Some Americans believed the Supreme Court had bent over backwards to protect the criminal but had forgotten the rights of the victim, and of society at large. Other Americans cheered the way the Supreme Court had defended the rights of the accused. If the *Escobedo* decision deepened a division already created by earlier

Supreme Court decisions, then the *Miranda* ruling would surely rip the country apart and create a valley between opponents in this constitutional clash.

Though the country was sharply divided, there could be no doubt that the *Powell, Brown, Gideon, Malloy,* and *Escobedo* decisions were all steppingstones for Ernesto Miranda. Each set a new precedent and shed new light on the interpretation of constitutional rights for the accused in a criminal case.

All of these cases were extremely important components of legal history in the United States. The *Escobedo* decision, a landmark case itself, would form a strong foundation for Miranda's appeal. As valuable as the *Escobedo* decision was for Miranda, however, differences between Miranda's case and Escobedo's would be a true challenge in Miranda's appeal to the United States Supreme Court.

Though the *Escobedo* case stood for the right of the accused to have an attorney present during interrogation, the facts of the *Miranda* case did not match Escobedo's. Escobedo had requested an attorney; records reflected that Miranda had not.[16] And many other differences existed between the *Miranda* and *Escobedo* cases. These differences would become key issues upon appeal in the legal battle between Miranda's lawyers and the lawyers representing the State of Arizona.

3

The Case for Miranda

Ernesto Miranda was twenty-three years old when he raped Rebecca Ann Johnson.[1] A life of crime was certainly nothing new to him. His difficulties had begun many years before.

Even as a child, Miranda led a troubled life. When he was six years old, his mother died. His father, a house painter, remarried the following year, and Miranda battled often with his stepmother. He soon lost close contact with his brothers, and with his father, whom he said had beaten him.

As a student at Queen of Peace Grammar School in Mesa, Arizona, Miranda was a nightmare for the nuns and priests. He was absent more than he was present, and he created more than his share of disciplinary problems.

In 1954, Miranda finished the eighth grade. That same year, he was arrested for his first felony, auto theft, for which he was put on probation. He returned to school the following year, but dropped out after completing only half of the ninth grade.

Miranda's probation did not seem to discourage him from a life of crime. In 1955, he was arrested for burglary and sentenced to serve time in the Arizona State Industrial School for Boys. The strict disciplinary measures at the State Boys' School did not stop Miranda from following a life of crime, either. He returned home in December of 1955, and one month later, he was arrested for rape and assault. He was sent back to the State Boys' School for one year.

Again, this time in jail did little, if anything, to prevent Miranda from continuing his life of crime. Between 1956 and 1961, he was convicted and imprisoned in Arizona, California, Texas, Tennessee, and Ohio for a variety of crimes. During that time, he served in the United States Army, where he went AWOL (absent without leave, or permission), much in line with his behavior in grammar school years before. His future brushes with the law would include a number of arrests for transporting cars across state lines. He would later say that he stole cars because he was "too lazy to work."

In 1962, Miranda was between jail sentences and

settled in the Phoenix, Arizona, area with Twila Hoffman. She would later prove to be his downfall in the second Rebecca Ann Johnson kidnap-rape trial.

Hoffman went to work in a nursery school while Miranda wove his way in and out of employment. He rarely held a job for more than two weeks. Finally, in August of 1962, Miranda got a job as a truck driver for a produce company. He was well thought of by his employer. Miranda and Hoffman had a baby girl, and it looked as though Miranda might settle down into the "straight and narrow."

This fleeting stability, however, would be shattered when it was learned that Miranda had returned to a life of crime. He had begun cruising the Phoenix area, where he committed a number of crimes against women. These included kidnap, rape, and robbery. The exact number of victims will never be known. Rebecca Ann Johnson was among them.[2]

On March 13, 1963, Miranda had worked all night long. One hour after he had arrived home and gone to sleep, Phoenix police officers Cooley and Young appeared at his door. They asked Miranda to accompany them to the police station to answer some questions about a case they were investigating. Miranda later explained, "I didn't know whether I had a choice. I got in the car and asked them what it was about. They said they couldn't tell me anything."[3]

At the police station, officers put Miranda in a lineup with three other men. Rebecca Ann was not able to identify any of them as her attacker, but she believed Miranda's build and features were similar to those of the man who had kidnapped and raped her. She asked if she could hear Miranda speak, believing that she could identify his voice.[4]

From the lineup, Miranda was taken to an interrogation room, where he asked officers, "How did I do?"

"You flunked," they answered.[5]

The interrogation had begun.

No attorney was present to protect Miranda's constitutional rights. Before the questioning began, Miranda was not told that he had the right to an attorney, and a dispute existed as to whether he had been told he had the right to remain silent.

Rebecca Ann Johnson was brought to the interrogation room, and officers asked Miranda to state his name and address so that Rebecca Ann could hear his voice. Officers then pointed to Rebecca Ann Johnson and asked Miranda, "Is that the girl?"

Believing that he had already been identified by the victim in the lineup, Miranda replied, "That's the girl."

As soon as Rebecca Ann heard Miranda's voice, she was certain that he was the man who had kidnapped and raped her.

During a relatively short interrogation period, Miranda not only confessed to the crime against Rebecca Ann Johnson, but admitted a robbery as well.

Officers were ready to get Miranda's statement in writing. They gave him a typed confession form. Near the top of the page appeared the statement:

> "I,_____, do hereby swear that I make this statement voluntarily and of my own free will, with no threats, coercion, or promises of immunity, and with full knowledge of my legal rights, understanding any statement I make may be used against me."

Miranda signed his name in the blank, wrote his confession, and signed at the bottom. Although the form stated that Miranda's confession was made with full knowledge of his rights, records reflect that officers did not explain exactly what those rights were.[6]

In June of 1963, the trial in the case of *The State of Arizona* v. *Ernesto Miranda* got under way in an Arizona state court. Miranda's lawyer, seventy-three-year-old Alvin Moore, had been appointed by the Court. He was paid $100.00 to defend Miranda in this case.[7]

In an attempt to prove that Miranda was insane, Moore asked the Court to appoint two psychiatrists to

7 3   6 0 0 0 2 7

Form 2000-66-D   **CITY OF PHOENIX, ARIZONA**   Witness/Suspect
Rev. Nov. 59   **POLICE DEPARTMENT**   Statement

SUBJECT: Rape   D.R. 63-08380

STATEMENT OF: ERNEST ARTHER MIRANDA

TAKEN BY: C Cooley #413 - W. Young #182

DATE: 3-13-63   TIME: 1³⁰/ Pm PLACE TAKEN: Interr Rm #2

I, _Ernest A Miranda_, do hereby swear that I make this statement voluntarily and of my own free will, with no threats, coercion, or promises of immunity, and with full knowledge of my legal rights, understanding any statement I make may be used against me.

I, _Ernest A Miranda_, am 23 years of age and have completed the _8th_ grade in school.

Seen a Girl walking up street stopped a little ahead of her got out of car walked towards her grabbed her by the arm and asked to get in the car. Got in car without force tied hands + ankles. . . . . . Drove her home . . . . . couldn't say I was sorry for what . . . . . her to say a prayer . . . . . AM.

I have read and understand the foregoing statement and hereby swear to its truthfulness.   _Ernest A Miranda_

WITNESS: _Carroll Cooley_
Wilfred M. Young #182

Miranda's confession was a key piece of evidence when he was first tried for the rape and kidnapping of Rebecca Ann Johnson.

examine his client. Neither found Miranda insane. The psychiatrists did, however, find that Miranda was immature and emotionally ill. Still, both doctors believed that he knew the difference between right and wrong. Their written opinions stated that Miranda knew the nature and consequences of his acts and that he was able to understand the proceedings against him and to assist in his own defense.[8]

Miranda's attorney expressed, in no uncertain terms, his repulsion in defending his client. He told the jury, "You know, perhaps a doctor doesn't enjoy operating for locked bowels, but he has to."[9]

Nonetheless, in order to provide proper legal representation for his client, Moore did object to the confession. He tried to keep Miranda's confession from being admitted as evidence, so that the jury could neither hear nor see it.

In doing so, Moore had to make a legal objection. The law generally requires that an attorney state the grounds, or legal basis, for an objection. Moore based his objection on the Sixth Amendment right to counsel. "We object because the Supreme Court of the United States says a man is entitled to an attorney at the time of his arrest," Moore stated.[10] This basis gave rise to Moore's argument that Miranda had a right to have a lawyer present during the interrogation, before the trial. In reality, the objection was inaccurate, as such a decision had not yet been made by the United States Supreme Court. No case existed which provided the rights Alvin Moore spoke of. The Supreme Court had ruled in the *Gideon* case, under the Sixth and Fourteenth Amendments, that the defendant had a right to a lawyer at the time of trial. But Moore had not based his objection on the right to a lawyer at the time of trial. And, though the *Escobedo* decision would deal with the right to a requested attorney before trial, that ruling had not yet come down from the Supreme Court. Indeed, the *Escobedo* decision would not be handed down until June of 1964.

When Officers Cooley and Young testified at Miranda's trial regarding the confession, they admitted that no explanation of rights had been given. Because they were aware that Miranda was an ex-convict, they believed that he knew his rights. Miranda had been through the "routine" before, lawyers would later argue, so there was no need to explain his rights in detail.

Further, Cooley and Young testified that neither threats nor promises had been made in exchange for Miranda's confession to the crime of rape, but simply and without coercion of any kind, they had questioned him. [11]

Miranda's account of his interrogation, though not stated at the trial, was quite different.

> Once they get you in a little room and they start badgering you one way or the other, "you better tell us . . . or we're going to throw the book at you" . . . that is what was told to me. They would throw the book at me. They would try to give me all the time they could. They thought there was even the possibility that there was something wrong with me. They would try to help me, get me medical care if I needed it . . . And I haven't had any sleep since the day before. I'm tired. I just got off work, and they have me and they are interrogating me. They mention first one crime, then another one, (sic) they are certain I am the person . . . knowing what a penitentiary is like, a person has to be frightened, scared. And not knowing if he'll be able to get back up and go home.[12]

When it was time for the judge in Miranda's trial to rule on the admissibility (whether evidence will be heard or excluded) of the confession, he allowed the confession into evidence.[13] This ruling meant that Moore's objection was overruled, and the jury was allowed to consider Miranda's confession when deciding whether to find him guilty or not guilty.

Miranda was convicted and sentenced to twenty-to-thirty years in prison. He was shipped off to the Arizona State Prison Farm. There he became best known as a barber, not as the celebrated "right-to-remain-silent man"

FEDERAL BUREAU OF INVESTIGATION, UNITED STATES DEPARTMENT OF JUSTICE

WASHINGTON, D.C.

CURRENT ARREST OR RECEIPT

DATE ARRESTED OR RECEIVED	CHARGE OR OFFENSE (If code citation is used it should be accompanied by charge)	DISPOSITION OR SENTENCE (List FINAL disposition only. If not now available, submit later on FBI Form R-84 for completion of record.)
7-5-1963 MARICOPA COUNTY	COUNT I-KIDNAPPING COUNT II-RAPE(FIRST DEGREE) TO RUN CONCURRENTLY	20 yrs.to 30 yrs.

OCCUPATION	RESIDENCE OF PERSON FINGERPRINTED
TRUCK DRIVER	WIFE: TWILA MIRANDA 157 E. COMMONWELL CHANDLER, ARIZONA

If COLLECT wire reply or COLLECT telephone reply is desired, indicate here

☐ Wire reply   ☐ Telephone reply

Telephone number

Sentence expires 7-5-1993

FOR INSTITUTIONS USE ONLY

INSTRUCTIONS

1. FORWARD ARREST CARDS TO FBI IMMEDIATELY AFTER FINGERPRINTING FOR MOST EFFECTIVE SERVICE.
2. TYPE or PRINT all information.
3. Note amputations in proper finger squares.
4. REPLY WILL QUOTE ONLY NUMBER APPEARING IN THE BLOCK MARKED "CONTRIBUTOR'S NO."
5. Indicate any additional copies for other agencies in space below—include their complete mailing address.

SEND COPY TO:

Joe M. Rodriguez, Secretary
ARIZONA STATE PRISON
Florence, Arizona

FD-249 (Rev. 4-27-62)

Officials at the state prison in Florence, Arizona received a copy of Miranda's FBI record.

he would become after his case had traveled to the highest court in the land.[14]

After the conviction in Arizona State trial court, Miranda's case was appealed to the Arizona Supreme Court. Miranda awaited the state supreme court's ruling from his prison cell. After almost a year and a half, the conviction was upheld, or left in place. The Arizona State Supreme Court stated that Miranda already knew his rights, since he was an ex-convict.[15]

After Miranda's case was affirmed by the Arizona Supreme Court, the American Civil Liberties Union (ACLU) became interested in Miranda's rights and the legal complexities of his case.

Robert Corcoran, the ACLU lawyer, was very concerned about Miranda's constitutional rights. According to Corcoran, an appeal to the United States Supreme Court was warranted. The *Escobedo* case, which stated that the suspect had the right to a requested attorney during questioning, would be an important aspect of the appeal.

After the *Escobedo* ruling, many unsuccessful attempts had been made to expand the constitutional rights of the accused. Attorney Corcoran, who would later become an Arizona Supreme Court Justice, believed that Ernesto Miranda's case might just be the appeal that could succeed in this attempt.[16]

Corcoran's frustration regarding the United States Supreme Court's failure to expand the rights of the accused mirrored the dissatisfaction of many Americans who wanted to see an expansion of the constitutional rights of the criminal suspect. The *Escobedo* decision had provided new rights for the accused, rights that had not existed before. Prior to *Escobedo*, the accused in a state court proceeding was entitled to an attorney at the time of trial—not before. In the *Escobedo* decision, the United States Supreme Court expanded the right to an attorney. This right became available at the time of interrogation, before the trial.

Even though, in the minds of those who supported expansion of rights of the accused, the *Escobedo* case had made a giant step forward in constitutional law, further steps were being met by a brick wall.

Though Miranda's attorney, Moore, was not in a position to handle his client's appeal to the United States Supreme Court, two other lawyers, John Flynn and John Frank, volunteered to take the case. Frank was a graduate of the Wisconsin and Yale Law Schools. He had served as a law clerk to United States Supreme Court Justice Hugo Black, and had taught in a law school. Flynn, a former World War II combat Marine was "acknowledged as one of the most astute criminal lawyers in the state [Arizona]."[17]

Flynn and Frank disagreed at first about the major legal point for the appeal. Flynn wanted to base the appeal on the Fifth Amendment privilege against self-incrimination. According to him, the circumstances surrounding Miranda's interrogation made the confession invalid. Upon appeal, he would put forth the position that Miranda was entitled to be made aware of his rights, that at the time of questioning the investigation had begun to focus on Miranda, and he should have had the opportunity to assert his Fifth Amendment privilege against self-incrimination.

Miranda's other lawyer, Frank, wanted to base the appeal on the Sixth Amendment right to counsel. His argument centered on the fact that, regardless of whether or not Miranda asked for an attorney, he had the right to representation at the time of questioning.

Ultimately, the Sixth Amendment position won out. The Sixth Amendment would be the basis for Ernesto Miranda's appeal to the Supreme Court of the United States.

It was true that the *Gideon* and *Escobedo* cases, which *had* been decided in time to be of benefit in Miranda's appeal, had not spelled out specifically that an accused must be advised of the right to an attorney prior to questioning. Still, Miranda's lawyers would make a strong appeal that the Sixth Amendment *did* provide that right and that the *Gideon* and *Escobedo* decisions had led the Court in this direction.[18]

Constitutional law is quite complex. Although the choice between Fifth Amendment and Sixth Amendment arguments might not always seem clear-cut, it is important for lawyers to choose a position upon which to base an appeal. Once the position has been chosen, attorneys can research the law as it relates to the specific points of the appeal. Only then can the lawyers discuss precedent to support their positions.

The brief, or written legal argument, for Miranda was clear and to the point. Miranda's lawyers framed their arguments in persuasive, simple, direct terms. The brief detailed Miranda's lineup and identification, his interrogation, and his confession. Lawyers discussed their opinions of the *Escobedo* decision as it applied to Miranda's case. They stated that the Arizona Supreme Court had given the *Escobedo* case "such a narrow construction that, for all practical purposes, the protections of the Sixth Amendment are not available to those persons so unaware of their rights or so intimidated that they do not request 'the guiding hand of counsel' at this crucial stage."

In addition, the lawyers stated their concern over giving "the knowledgeable suspect . . . a constitutional preference over those members of society most in need of assistance." The lawyers were concerned that certain members of society who are wealthy or well-educated might have an "edge" over those who are poor and illiterate. The wealthy and well-educated would likely know that they should request an attorney. The poor and illiterate, who truly need the protection of the Constitution, might not be aware of their rights.

Miranda's lawyers also addressed the confusion that had arisen among lawyers, police officers, judges, and others as a result of the *Escobedo* decision and its limited application. The confusion had given rise to many questions, questions that were ringing out across the country. When exactly does the right to an attorney arise? At the time of trial? During interrogation? Prior to interrogation? At the time of the arrest? Does the accused have the constitutional right to be advised of the right to an attorney? If so, when?

Frank and Flynn asked, in their brief, whether "the confession of a poorly educated, mentally abnormal, indigent defendant, not told of his right to counsel, taken while he is in police custody and without the assistance of counsel, which was never requested, can be admitted into evidence over specific objection based on the absence of counsel?"

The lawyers went on to discuss past cases which had dealt with issues such as the coerced confession and the right to counsel. They brought up cases such as *Powell* v. *Alabama*, *Brown* v. *Mississippi*, and *Gideon* v. *Wainwright*. Particularly, the lawyers quoted from the *Powell* v. *Alabama* decision, stating that, under the due process clause of the Fourteenth Amendment, the criminal defendant was entitled to the "guiding hand of counsel in every step of the proceedings against him."

Flynn and Frank stated that Miranda's life "was for all practical purposes over" when he left the interrogation room. They argued that waiting until the time of trial to appoint an attorney for suspects in situations like Miranda's was "meaningless" because results of interrogation could be so harmful that even the most skilled attorney would be of little help at a point as late as the trial.

And so, the lawyers argued, the question at hand was whether the Sixth Amendment right to counsel, as applied to the states through the Fourteenth Amendment, gave the same right to have counsel at interrogation as at the time of trial. In answering this question, Flynn and Frank stated that this right did exist, not as the result of the *Escobedo* ruling, or of any other single case, but rather because "there is a tide in the affairs of men, and it is this engulfing tide which is washing away the secret interrogation of the unprotected accused."

The *Escobedo* opinion, Miranda's lawyers argued, did

apply beyond its fact situation because it had already recognized the interrogation as a proceeding covered by the Sixth Amendment. Thus, the indigent suspect did have the right to counsel during interrogation, whether counsel had been requested or not.

Frank and Flynn discussed the opposing position that, if the Court decided that indigent suspects were entitled to counsel at the interrogation stage, then the police would be "handcuffed" and would not be able to successfully perform their law enforcement duties. The lawyers had researched many opinions on this point. They noted that there was a great division of opinion across the country. The attorneys offered a summary of both points of view. They quoted a district attorney, someone directly involved in law enforcement, who had stated, ". . . Changes in court decisions and prosecution procedure would have about the same effect on the crime rate as an aspirin would have on a tumor of the brain . . ."

Flynn and Frank closed their brief with a powerful point: "We invoke the basic principles of *Powell* v. *Alabama*: 'He requires the guiding hand of counsel at every step in the proceeding against him.' When Miranda stepped into Interrogation Room 2, he had only the guiding hand of Officers Cooley and Young."[19]

Miranda's attorneys had made their arguments. The lawyer for the state of Arizona had a few of his own.

4

The Case for the State of Arizona

Months before Ernesto Miranda's trial, prosecutors in the Maricopa County Attorney's Office in Phoenix, Arizona, received police reports regarding the kidnap-rape of Rebecca Ann Johnson.[1] Reports were sent to his office because a criminal case is generally prosecuted in the county where the crime occurred, and in this case the incident happened in Maricopa County.

Lawyers working in the county attorney's office represent the people of the state of Arizona. The victims in their criminal cases are referred to as "complaining witnesses" and do not have to pay a fee for representation. This money is generally paid through tax dollars. Rebecca Ann Johnson was the complaining witness in the *Miranda* case.

Before the trial, prosecutors had at their disposal over twenty pages of police reports, not to mention the many other records in the case.[2] Miranda had been convicted of robbery the day before his trial in the Rebecca Ann Johnson kidnap-rape case. He had confessed to that robbery at the same time he confessed to the kidnap-rape.[3]

On June 20, 1963, Ernesto Miranda's trial for the kidnap-rape of Rebecca Ann Johnson began. Attorneys chose the jury members and began presenting testimony, questioning witnesses.

Prosecutors questioned a total of four witnesses: complaining witness Rebecca Ann Johnson, Rebecca Ann's sister, and Officers Cooley and Young.[4]

Rebecca Ann Johnson was the first witness called to the stand. She sometimes had to stop speaking and take a break since her voice was trembling.[5] She did, however, from the witness stand, identify Ernesto Miranda in court as the man who had kidnapped and raped her.

After Rebecca Ann stepped down from the stand, her sister testified. Her sister's testimony centered on Rebecca Ann's condition at the time she had arrived home. "She came home, pounded on the door, her hair was all over like she had been in a fight, and her dress was brand new, a new suit, and it was a mess, and she was crying and carrying on, and I asked her what was the matter . . ." Rebecca Ann's sister was questioned only briefly by the prosecutor. Miranda's lawyer asked her no questions.

The prosecutor next called Officer Cooley, and then Officer Young to the stand. They testified for quite some time, detailing the crime as it had been described to them. They also testified as to the lineup and Miranda's confession.

On cross-examination, Miranda's lawyer asked about how the confession had been obtained:

Question: Did you warn him of his rights?

Answer: Yes, Sir.

Question: But did you ever, before or during your conversation or before taking this statement, did you ever advise the defendant he was entitled to the services of an attorney?

Answer: When I read—

Question: Before he made any statement?

Answer: When I read the statement right there.

Question: I don't see in the statement that it says where he is entitled to the services of an attorney before he made it.

Answer: No, sir.

Question: Is it not in that statement?

Answer: It doesn't say anything about an attorney . . .

Question: . . . It is not your practice to advise people

you arrest that they are entitled to the services of an attorney before they make a statement?

Answer: No, sir.

Moore, Miranda's court-appointed lawyer, tried to keep the jury from hearing the confession, objecting on the grounds that his client's rights had been violated because Miranda had not had an attorney present at the time the confession was made. The objection was overruled, and the jury was allowed to consider the confession.

Miranda's lawyer presented no defense witnesses; Miranda did not take the stand. The prosecutor and the defense attorney made their final arguments to the jury.

All in all, the trial had been quite short, and the legal arguments had been confined to a minimum amount of time.

After the final arguments, the judge instructed the jury about the law. He told the jurors that in order to convict Miranda, they would have to find that the state had proven its case beyond a reasonable doubt.[6]

"Beyond a reasonable doubt" is the burden of proof required of the prosecution in a criminal case. It is more difficult to prove a criminal case than a civil case, as the winning side in a civil trial generally receives only monetary compensation. In a criminal case, however, a person can be deprived of liberty and can be left with a criminal record. A remarkable difference exists between giving up money and giving up freedom.

In the civil case, the burden of proof is "by a preponderance of the evidence." This phrase simply means that, if the evidence in each side's case were placed on a scale, the side that weighed more would win. Thus, we have the expression "tipping the scales of justice." In a criminal case, however, the burden of proof is more strict.

Many people believe that a criminal case must be proven "beyond a shadow of a doubt." This idea has been promoted by television shows and movies, but it is not the standard used by the courts. In order to believe a case beyond a shadow of a doubt, a jury would, at the very least, need to view a videotape of a crime. Except in the rarest or most bizarre of circumstances, this simply does not happen. And the prosecutor cannot physically return the jurors to the crime scene on the date at the time the offense occurred.

There is no universally accepted definition of the phrase "beyond a reasonable doubt." Both the prosecutor and the defense attorney have an opportunity to argue whether sufficient evidence exists to meet the burden of proof.

In the *Miranda* trial, the judge instructed the jury regarding the burden of proof in this way:

A reasonable doubt is not a mere whim or guess or imaginary doubt, nor is it a mere subterfuge [trick] to which resort may be held in order to avoid doing a disagreeable thing. It is such a doubt as reasonable men may entertain after a careful and honest review and consideration of all the evidence in the case. It must be founded in reason and common sense.

The rule of law to which I refer does not require that the defendant be proven guilty beyond all doubt, because in many cases that would be an impossibility. There is nothing human probably that can be said to be beyond all doubt. The law says that the defendant is entitled to the benefit of a reasonable doubt, not all doubt . . .

Regarding Miranda's failure to testify in the trial, the judge instructed the jury:

It is a constitutional right of a defendant in a criminal trial that he may not be compelled to testify. Thus whether or not he does testify rests entirely in his own decision. The failure of a defendant to deny or explain evidence against him does not create a presumption of guilt, nor does it relieve the prosecution of its burden of proving every essential element of the crime and the guilt of the defendant beyond a reasonable doubt.

The judge went on to instruct the jurors regarding the law as it relates to confessions. The jurors were told that it was their job to determine whether Ernesto Miranda's confession had been made voluntarily. If so, the confession could be considered.

If, however, the jurors found the confession to have been made involuntarily, they were told that they must entirely disregard it and not consider it for any purpose. The judge went on to state:

> A confession is involuntary when it is obtained by any sort of violence or threats, or by any direct or implied promises of immunity [protection] or benefit, or by any improper influence which might induce in the mind of the defendant, the belief or hope that he would gain or benefit or be better off by making a statement, and where the defendant makes such confession as a result of any such inducement originating with a law enforcement officer. But the fact that a defendent was under arrest at the time he made a confession or that he was not at the time represented by Counsel or that he was not told that any statement that he might make could or would be used against him, in and of themselves, will not render such confession involuntary.[7]

After deliberating, discussing the case in the jury room, for five hours, the nine-man, three-woman jury returned to the courtroom with a verdict. Ernesto Miranda was pronounced guilty of kidnap and rape.

Miranda was sent to the county jail to await his sentencing. The following week, on June 27, 1963, Ernesto Miranda was summoned from jail to the courtroom. The judge sentenced him to not less than twenty years, nor more than thirty years on the kidnap conviction. He was sentenced to the same punishment, twenty to thirty years, on the rape conviction. The two sentences would, however, run concurrently, so Miranda would be serving time in prison for both offenses at the

In The Superior Court
Maricopa County, Arizona

THE STATE OF ARIZONA.
Plaintiff,

vs.

ERNEST ARTHUR MIRANDA

Defendant.

Div- 10 Judge McFate

Criminal Case No. 41948

JUDGMENT OF GUILT AND SENTENCE

On the ....27th........day of.................................June................, 1963...., the hereinafter named defendant personally appeared before the court (without an attorney) (with his attorney) ....Alvin Moore..

The State of Arizona was represented by (Deputy) County Attorney..

The following proceedings were had:

The defendant was informed that .....he had heretofore (entered a plea of guilty to) (been tried and found guilty of) the offense specified in this judgment, which the defendant acknowledged to be correct. The following judgment of guilt was then entered in the presence of the defendant:

IT IS THE JUDGMENT of the court that the defendant...Ernest Arthur Miranda............................
is guilty of..........COUNT I-KIDNAPPING, AND COUNT II:RAPE (First Degree) Felonies.............
as charged in (Count...........of) the...(Information) (Complaint) (Indictment).

The defendant was asked whether .....he had anything to say or any legal cause to show why sentence should not be pronounced. There was none.

as to Count I

IT IS THE JUDGMENT AND SENTENCE OF THE COURT, that the defendant be serve a term in the Arizona State Prison at Florence, Arizona, of not less than twenty (20) years nor more than Thirty (30) years; and that on Count II, that you serve a term in the Arizona State Prison, at Florence, Arizona, of not less than Twenty (20) years nor more than Thirty (30) years, said sentences on Counts I and II to run concurrently. Defendant is remanded to the Sheriff.

The judgment and sentence document is generally made a part of public record after a defendant's conviction.

same time and his total sentence in the Rebecca Ann Johnson crime would be twenty to thirty years.

Also on June 27, 1963, Ernesto Miranda was sentenced in his robbery case. He received a sentence of twenty to twenty-five years. The judge pronounced that this sentence would run consecutively to (immediately following) the kidnap-rape sentence. Thus, Miranda would be sentenced to a total of not less than forty nor more than fifty-five years in prison for the crimes against the robbery victim and Rebecca Ann Johnson.

Miranda's lawyer filed notice of intention to appeal both the robbery and the kidnap-rape convictions to the Arizona Supreme Court.[8] While Miranda's lawyer argued to the state supreme court that his client's convictions should be reversed, the lawyers for the state of Arizona strongly urged the convictions be affirmed.

The state's position was that Ernesto Miranda's confession had been voluntary and that no law existed which required that officers offer an attorney to a suspect prior to questioning. The Arizona Supreme Court agreed with the state's attorney, and on April 22, 1965, Miranda's conviction was upheld.

In examining the Sixth and Fourteenth Amendments and their guarantees, the Arizona Supreme Court spoke of the balance necessary "between the competing interests of society and the rights of the individual . . . Society has the right of protection against those who roam the streets for the purpose of violating the law, but that protection must not be at the expense of the rights of the individual guaranteed under the Sixth and Fourteenth Amendments to our Constitution."

The Court emphasized, however, that Miranda had not been deprived of his constitutional rights. He had not asked for an attorney. This point was a critical one in the comparison between the United States Supreme Court's *Escobedo* decision and the facts in Ernesto Miranda's case. The Arizona Supreme Court went on to state that Miranda had "a record which indicated that he was not without courtroom experience" and that "he was certainly not unfamiliar with legal procedure and his rights in court."[9]

After the Arizona Supreme Court upheld Miranda's convictions, John Flynn and John Frank appealed the kidnap-rape case to the United States Supreme Court. When Miranda's lawyers took his kidnap-rape case to the United States Supreme Court, they decided it was not necessary to take the same steps in the robbery case. They did not appeal that case. Their reasoning was well-founded. If the Justices reversed the conviction in the kidnap-rape, surely the conviction in the robbery case would not stand, as Miranda had confessed to both cases at the same time, under the same circumstances.[10]

After Miranda's appeal to the United States Supreme Court in the kidnap-rape case was filed, notice was sent to the Arizona Attorney General's Office, the office that handled appeals for the people of the state of Arizona. In the Criminal Appeals Division of the Arizona Attorney General's Office, only one assistant attorney general and a couple of law clerks handled the appeals for the state. The assistant attorney general who handled the case of *Miranda* v. *Arizona* was Gary Nelson.

Nelson had graduated from law school only three years before. Still, he was highly regarded, having received many honors for speaking and academic skills.[11]

It was Nelson's responsibility to handle the response of the state of Arizona to Ernesto Miranda's appeal to the Supreme Court of the United States. Nelson had no objection to the United States Supreme Court hearing the *Miranda* case. He agreed with Flynn and Frank that the legal issues presented in Miranda's case had been a source of confusion. He further stated, however, that the rights granted to the accused in the *Escobedo* case should not be expanded. Nelson held firm to his position: The ruling in the *Escobedo* case did not give a suspect the right to have an attorney present at the time of questioning. Miranda's constitutional rights had not been violated.

In further distinguishing the *Miranda* case from the *Escobedo* case, Nelson was quick to point out that, in the

Escobedo case, the defendant had asked for an attorney. Miranda had made no such request, and as a result, the Phoenix police had not made a legal error by failing to provide an attorney. In addition, Nelson stated that Escobedo had not had experience with the police, whereas Miranda had an extensive criminal record.

Nelson added that Ernesto Miranda had been questioned only by police officers in a "routine investigation." Escobedo's interrogation had been carried out by police officers and a bright state's attorney.

Nelson went on to note that Escobedo had been "tricked" into confessing when told that another person had identified him as being the man who had pulled the trigger. He pointed out that in Miranda's case, on the other hand, police officers had not used tricks.[12]

Whether or not the police officers had used tricks with Miranda was, of course, debatable. After the lineup, officers told Miranda that he had "flunked," when, in fact, he hadn't. Further, officers asked Miranda, "Is that the girl?" These tactics could be viewed as tricks.

Assistant Attorney General Nelson addressed the issue of advice given to suspects regarding constitutional rights. Escobedo had been given none. Miranda, however, had agreed in his statement that he understood his rights and waived them.

Certainly, the United States Supreme Court would

consider the fact that, although Miranda signed a statement advising he was aware of his rights, these rights were never specified. He was not told that he had the right to have an attorney present. Records reflected that he was not told that he had a right to remain silent, though this matter was later disputed. It was the position of the state of Arizona, however, that these warnings simply were not necessary.

It was further the position of the state of Arizona that constitutional protections did not exist for the purpose of giving the guilty special chances for acquittal, being found "not guilty." Nelson argued:

> [Miranda] it seems, would have us interpret our adversary system of criminal justice as giving the accused a right to "win" the contest. While it may be inherent in the very nature of our system, with its vital and essential safeguards to individual freedom, that a person who actually commits a criminal act may have extra opportunities to escape punishment for his crime, it must be clear that the intent of the Constitutional safeguards were to insure, as much as humanly possible, that the innocent and unpopular would not be wrongfully harassed, intimidated or convicted—not that the guilty should have any special chances for acquittal or other favorable result.

Furthermore, Nelson was particularly provoked by a specific comment Miranda's lawyers had made in their brief: "[Miranda] states his life, for all practical purposes, was over when he walked out of Interrogation Room #2 on March 13, 1963."

Nelson replied, in the state's brief,: "The real fact is that Miranda's life was unalterably destined ten days earlier during the late evening hours of March 2 and the early morning hours of March 3, when he kidnapped and raped his victim . . ."[13] Nelson's reply illustrated his irritation with blaming police officers for Ernesto Miranda's fate, and his belief that Miranda had determined his own destiny by committing the crimes against Rebecca Ann Johnson.

Miranda's lawyers, John Flynn and John Frank, had dynamically presented the appeal on behalf of their client, Ernesto Miranda. Assistant Attorney General Gary Nelson had supported his position on behalf of the people of the state of Arizona.

Now the case of *Ernesto Miranda* v. *The State of Arizona* was in the hands of the nine Justices of the Supreme Court of the United States.

5

The Decision

On June 13, 1966, the Supreme Court handed down its decision in the *Miranda* case. This ruling fed the fires of controversy blazing around the rights of the criminal versus the rights of the victim and society. Indeed, the Supreme Court decision was made by the smallest possible margin, five to four.

Ernesto Miranda's name became entwined with legal history almost as the luck of the draw. His case was actually ruled upon along with three others, due to the fact that all four cases involved essentially the same legal issues. Of these four cases, Miranda's was listed first because he was the first to formally request that the United States Supreme Court hear his case.[1] So, the Supreme Court decision in regard to Ernesto Miranda,

Michael Vignera, Carl Calvin Westover, and Roy Allen Stewart came to be known in the history books, in the police departments, in the courtrooms, and on the streets across the country as the *Miranda* decision.

In 1966, the time was ripe for a ruling on legal issues like those presented in Miranda's case. Why then, did the Supreme Court Justices have to wait for Miranda's appeal to come to them? Why could the Justices not set down the law as they believed it should be?

It is true that the Supreme Court does make law when it hands down decisions. Supreme Court Justices cannot, however, simply decide to make rules of law. Rather, a "case or controversy" must exist. This means that the Justices must wait for an appropritate case to come to them in order to be able to rule on a particular area of the law.

Initially, Ernesto Miranda's case was decided at the state court level, where he was convicted. He appealed to the Arizona Supreme Court, where his conviction was upheld. Then Miranda personally made a request from his prison cell that the United States Supreme Court hear his case. Such a request is called a petition for writ of certiorari.

When Miranda sent his petition, he filed a pauper's form, which stated that he had little or no money and could not pay the $100 filing fee. Filing a pauper's form also meant that Miranda would be required to furnish only one petition to the United States Supreme Court, rather than the usually-required forty copies.

Unfortunately, Miranda forgot to attach a statement of his inability to pay. He also forgot to attach another important document—the final judgment of the Arizona Supreme Court. As both documents were required by law, Miranda's petition was dismissed.[2]

A short time later, Arizona attorneys John Flynn and John Frank agreed to represent Miranda on a pro bono, or at no charge, basis. As it turned out, the lawyers contributed over $50,000 in office time alone, not including their printing costs, travel time, and additional expenses.

When Flynn and Frank agreed to represent Miranda, he sent them a letter of thanks.[3] Little could Ernesto Miranda have known when he wrote that letter that these two lawyers would take his case to the highest heights in United States legal history.

After Miranda's lawyers and lawyers in many other cases had submitted petitions for writ of certiorari, the Supreme Court Justices began the process of deciding which cases they would hear. These were the cases in which they would grant certiorari. At the time the petition in the *Miranda* case was submitted, the Justices had asked their clerks to seek out *Escobedo*-type cases,

cases that dealt with the right to an attorney. The Justices were concerned with the confusion in the country following the *Escobedo* decision.

Were the criminal suspect's constitutional rights to be expanded? After the *Escobedo* ruling, law enforcement officers knew they must provide an attorney if one were requested. But what if one had not been requested? When exactly did the right to an attorney arise? These and many other questions were being asked by people throughout the nation.[4]

Up until the *Miranda* ruling, the Supreme Court had narrowly interpreted the *Escobedo* decision. As a result, those appellants, people appealing their cases, whose fact situations were not parallel to Escobedo's were generally not receiving reversals of their convictions. The decisions of the state courts were allowed to stand. Those Americans on the "law and order" side of the controversy expressed approval, while those Americans on the "suspect's rights" side anxiously awaited the day when criminal suspects' constitutional rights would be made broader.

On November 22, 1965, the Supreme Court of the United States granted certiorari in Miranda's case. Shortly thereafter, the Court also agreed to hear the cases of Michael Vignera, Carl Calvin Westover, and Roy Allen Stewart—the three men whose cases were similar to

Miranda's. The Court then requested briefs from the lawyers in those cases.

The brief is different from the petition for writ of certiorari which Miranda's lawyers had sent earlier to the Supreme Court. The petition for writ of certiorari explains why the Supreme Court should hear a case. The brief is a document which advocates a particular position. It explains why the Supreme Court should decide for a particular party to the case.

Over 700 pages of briefs were filed in the United States Supreme Court case of *Ernesto Miranda* v. *Arizona*. Though Miranda's lawyers filed a concise brief, many other briefs came to the Court in this case. A number of them were amicus curiae, or friends of the court, briefs.[5] These are briefs filed by people who are not parties to the case but who believe they have important comments to make before a ruling is handed down.

On Monday, February 2, 1966, Miranda's lawyers and the lawyers for the state of Arizona appeared before the Justices of the Supreme Court of the United States for oral argument. These are arguments the lawyers actually stand up and make in person to the Justices of the Supreme Court.

Miranda's lawyers had agreed they would base their argument on the Sixth Amendment right to counsel. As the oral arguments proceeded, however, it became clear

John Flynn, John Frank, Gary Nelson, and many others argued the *Miranda* case in the courtroom of the Supreme Court of the United States.

that the Justices were interested in a discussion of the Fifth Amendment privilege against self-incrimination.

When one of the Justices asked Flynn, Miranda's lawyer, if the right to a lawyer existed during the interrogation, when the investigation had begun to focus on the accused, Flynn said, "I think that the man at that time has the right to exercise, if he knows, and under the present state of the law in Arizona, if he's rich enough, and if he's educated enough, to assert his Fifth Amendment right, and if he recognizes he has a Fifth Amendment right, to request counsel."

After that comment and several others by Flynn, one of the Justices asked if the right to an attorney existed at the time of interrogation, then did every other constitutional right also come into play? Would it then be required that a jury be brought into the interrogation room?

Flynn replied that, certainly, a jury would not be required, that a ruling on Miranda's behalf "would simply extend those constitutional rights which police are about to take away from him." Later in the argument, Flynn would say that Miranda "was called upon to surrender a right that he didn't fully realize and appreciate that he had."

When Flynn was questioned about what a lawyer would advise, if a lawyer were available during questioning, he responded that a lawyer would advise that the accused had the right not to incriminate himself, the right not to make any statement, the right to be free from further questioning by the police department, the right at the ultimate time to be represented adequately by counsel, and that if the accused were too poor to employ counsel, the state would employ counsel for him. Flynn went on to state that the accused had "the right not to be convicted out of his own mouth."

When asked, "Why does the [Fifth] Amendment not protect the rich as well as the poor, the literate as well as the illiterate," Flynn responded:

> I'd say that it [the Fifth Amendment] certainly and most assuredly . . . does protect the rich, the educated, the strong, those rich enough to hire counsel, those who are educated enough to know what their rights are, those who are strong enough to withstand police questioning and assert those rights . . .

At that point, one of the Justices said, "I'm asking you only about Fifth Amendment provisions, 'No person shall be compelled to be a witness against himself.' Does that protection [apply] to every person or just some persons . . . I'm talking about what the Amendment is supposed to do."

Flynn replied, "It is supposed to apply to all persons."

When Flynn's allotted time for oral argument was up, the lawyer for the state of Arizona, Gary Nelson, stood up to offer his oral argument. His position, of course, was that Miranda's conviction should be upheld.

Nelson argued, "The practical effect of introducing counsel at the interrogation stage is going to stop the interrogation for any and all purposes except what counsel decides will be in the best interest of his defendant. Otherwise counsel will not be doing his job."

The question immediately following from the Court was very interesting: "Isn't that about the same thing as the practical effect and object of the Amendment which says 'He shall not be compelled to testify against himself'? Is there any difference between the object, the purposes . . . what the lawyer tells him and what the Fifth Amendment [provides]? . . . Isn't that the object of the Amendment?"

Nelson's next comment was surprising. It almost sounded as if he were arguing for Miranda.

> . . . The pre-trial police interrogation does more than just develop confessions; it develops incriminating statements. It develops . . . statements which pin a suspect down very closely after the crime has been committed, or very closely after he's been taken into police custody which prevent or . . . make it unprofitable for him to perjure himself or change his testimony at the trial.

To that comment, one of the Justices asked, "Is there anything fantastic in the idea that the Fifth Amendment protection against being compelled to testify against one's self might be read reasonably as meaning there should be no pre-trial proceedings when he was there in the possession of the state?"[6]

Perhaps the lawyers had a feel for how the Justices might rule in this case.

On the afternoon of March 2, 1966, several days after the oral arguments had begun, they were finished, and the Court moved on to arguments in another case.

In arriving at its decision in the *Miranda* opinion, the Court looked to the history of confession law as it had evolved in the United States. The opinion discussed, in great detail, the "overzealous police practices" of the past, those practices involving physical brutality.

Specifically, a New York case was mentioned. ". . . the police brutally beat, kicked, and placed lighted cigarette butts on the back of a potential witness under interrogation for the purpose of securing a statement incriminating a third party."

Chief Justice Warren, writing for the majority in his opinion, was clearly outraged at the brutal methods used in the past to coerce confessions. He stated that, though cases of this nature had definitely become the exception, they still existed in sufficient number to be of concern. He believed that something needed to be done to assure that this behavior would be stopped altogether.

The Supreme Court discussed a passage from the

Wickersham Report (discussed in Chapter Two). The following was included:

> Not only does the use of the third degree involve a flagrant violation of law by the officers of the law, but it involves the danger of false confessions, and it tends to make police and prosecutors less zealous in the search for objective evidence. As the New York prosecutor quoted in the report said, "It is a short cut and makes the police lazy and unenterprising." Or as another official quoted remarked: "If you use your fists, you are not so likely to use your wits."

The Court's opinion went on to discuss the fact that the practice of in-custody interrogation had generally become psychologically rather than physically oriented. The Court examined current published guides of police practice. Among them, perhaps, dwelled the strategy used on Ernesto Miranda.

The Supreme Court detailed many tactics recommended in the manuals. The Court discussed the "Mutt and Jeff" strategy, where one officer would act friendly and the other would act just the opposite. Another interrogation device examined was the ploy in which officers would advise a suspect that an identification had been made by a number of witnesses when, in fact, no such identification had been made. Privacy was the key element to a successful interrogation, these manuals taught.

Additionally, the manuals referred to in the Supreme

Court decision directed that an interrogator's comments should center on *why* the suspect had committed the crime rather than on *whether* the suspect had committed the crime.

In the Supreme Court opinion, the Justices detailed specific procedures recommended in police manuals:

> In the event that the subject wishes to speak to a relative or an attorney, the following advice is tendered [given]:
>
> "The interrogator should respond by suggesting the subject first tell the truth to the interrogator himself rather than get anyone else involved in the matter. If the request is for an attorney, the interrogator may suggest that the subject save himself or his family the expense of such professional service, particularly if he is innocent of the offense under investigation. The interrogator may also add, 'Joe, I'm only looking for the truth, and if you're telling the truth, that's it. You can handle this by yourself.'"
>
> "When normal procedures fail to produce the needed result, the police may resort to deceptive [strategies] such as giving false legal advice. It is important to keep the subject off balance, for example, by trading on his insecurity about himself or his surroundings. The police then persuade, trick, or cajole him out of exercising his constitutional rights . . ."[7]

Chief Justice Earl Warren, the author of the *Miranda* Supreme Court opinion, was obviously incensed at the methods designed to "trick" suspects into confessing. He stated, "The current practice of incommunicado interrogation is at odds with one of our Nation's most cherished principles—that the individual may not be compelled to incriminate himself."[8] Justice Warren was, of course, speaking of Fifth Amendment rights.

After discussing confession law at length, the Supreme Court opinion examined the *Escobedo* case and its significance in the *Miranda* ruling.

As might have been predicted, in the *Miranda* decision the Supreme Court decided to expand the *Escobedo* ruling, stating that the Fifth Amendment privilege against self-incrimination was available prior to criminal court proceedings and that a suspect must be told of the right to an attorney. After the *Miranda* decision, "suspects would be afforded the right to counsel in any situation in which freedom of action was curtailed in any significant way."

It is a common belief that the Supreme Court set forth in its decision the specific wording required of the *Miranda* warning; however, this is not the case. The actual comment in the Supreme Court decision is:

> Prior to any questioning, the person must be warned that he has a right to remain silent, that any statement he does make may be used as evidence against him, and that he has a right to the presence of an attorney, either retained [hired and paid for by the defendant] or appointed [hired by the court and generally paid by the state].[9]

The Supreme Court opinion went on to state that the defendant could waive or exercise these rights under the

Miranda ruling at any time prior to or during the questioning. This means that if a defendant has begun to give a statement, but then decides to request an attorney, the questioning must stop immediately and an attorney must be provided.

One practical result of the *Miranda* ruling has been the use of "warning cards" by police. Though the wording of the *Miranda* warning may vary from state to state, law enforcement officers generally carry a card or a sheet of paper with a specific warning to advise suspects of their rights. Common wording includes:

> You have the right to remain silent.
> Anything you say can and will be used against you in a court of law.
> You have the right to the presence of an attorney to assist you during questioning, if you so desire.
> If you cannot afford an attorney, you have the right to have an attorney appointed for you prior to questioning.
> Do you understand these rights?

When the Supreme Court reversed Miranda's conviction in the kidnap-rape case, Flynn and Frank believed that Miranda's conviction in the robbery case could not be left in place, as the confessions in both cases had been made at the same time, under the same circumstances. This was not to be, as the Supreme Court decided that the *Miranda* ruling was not retroactive. It did not apply to cases decided before the Supreme

Court's *Miranda* decision. Lawyers did, however, through complex legal work, later manage to get the original robbery conviction reversed. Even so, Miranda was later retried and convicted on the robbery charge.[10]

Though the famous *Miranda* warning came as a result of the United States Supreme Court's opinion in the *Miranda* case, not all Supreme Court Justices agreed with the decision. When a Supreme Court opinion is handed down, it becomes law. However, Justices in the minority, or those Justices who disagree with the majority, have the opportunity to publish dissenting, or disagreeing, opinions. Although these dissenting opinions are published with the majority opinion, they do not become law.

It is interesting to note, however, that the dissenting opinions can sometimes predict a trend in the Supreme Court. Indeed, the majority position in the *Miranda* case might have been predictable from earlier dissents. In many of these earlier dissents, where the majority opinion had failed to expand the rights of the accused, the dissenting Justices expressed opinions similar to the majority opinion in the *Miranda* ruling. Thus, a majority of Justices finally came to rule in a way consistent with the expansion of the rights of the accused.

Being decided by the smallest margin possible, it is not surprising that *Miranda* sparked a number of dissents. These dissenting opinions mirrored beliefs held by many people involved in law enforcement.

Justice Tom C. Clark, in his dissent, expressed his opinion of the *Miranda* ruling in this way: "Such a strict constitutional specific inserted at the nerve center of crime detection may well kill the patient."[11] Clark, along with other critics, believed that the *Miranda* ruling might well destroy the criminal justice system. In addition, Clark and those with similar beliefs felt that the Supreme Court had gone too far in expanding the rights of the accused while not properly respecting the rights of the victim and of society at large.

And what happened to Ernesto Miranda after the United States Supreme Court overturned his conviction in the kidnap-rape case? Miranda was ready to celebrate when he heard the news. He believed that he would soon walk out of prison a free man, but this was not to be. Though Miranda's conviction had been reversed, the state of Arizona still had the right to go to trial again on his case in Arizona state court. Ernesto Miranda would have to wait in custody for that trial.[12]

In the second trial, the "fruit of the poisonous tree" would be excluded from evidence, meaning that Miranda's confession could not be heard by the jury. The term "fruit of the poisonous tree" is used to describe a piece of evidence that has come from an illegal procedure. Because the procedure was illegal to begin with, and because the evidence against the defendant may not be used at trial, the evidence is called "fruit of the poisonous tree." Thus, because Miranda's interrogation was illegal, his confession could not be used in court.

John Flynn prepared for Miranda's second trial, which was scheduled to begin on October 24, 1966, but the trial had to be postponed because Rebecca Ann Johnson was pregnant and due to have her baby in November. After Miranda's first trial, Rebecca Ann Johnson had gone about the business of living. She had gotton married and had a child. She was expecting her second.[13]

Finally, on February 15, 1967 almost four years after the crime, Miranda's second trial began. The prosecution had a tough case on its hands. By this time, there were legal questions as to whether Rebecca Ann could identify Ernesto Miranda as the man who had kidnapped and raped her. Miranda's lawyer questioned the validity of Rebecca Ann's identification of Miranda from years before. The lawyer raised many issues regarding her identification of Miranda at the police station, after the lineup. In addition, the jury would not be allowed to hear or see Miranda's confession.

Perhaps Miranda realized what a difficult case this was for the prosecution. He was described as "composed and detached, even slightly amused at times," during the six-hour voir dire, questioning of possible jurors.[14]

Miranda may have been dismayed, however, at the testimony given by the prosecution's key witness, Twila Hoffman. Hoffman was the mother of Miranda's child and the woman he had been living with at the time he committed Rebecca Ann Johnson's kidnap and rape.

Some reports state that Twila Hoffman came forward to prosecutors and police because Miranda had reported her to Welfare authorities and was trying to take their daughter away from her. These same reports state that Miranda had admitted the kidnap-rape to Hoffman during a prison visit and that Miranda had asked Hoffman to offer his hand in marriage to Rebecca Ann Johnson.[15]

Moise Berger, one of the prosecutors in the second *Miranda* trial, describes what actually happened in interviews with Twila Hoffman. Berger says that Hoffman did not come to prosecutors and police at all. Rather, he, as the prosecutor in the case, found Hoffman. Berger says that he knew the second trial would be tough, that "it would come down to [Rebecca Ann's] word against Ernie's." And so, Berger really needed more. Flynn, Miranda's lawyer, was out looking for more witnesses, and Berger did the same. Berger said, "I figured he would probably contact Ernie's girlfriend."

As it turned out, the prosecution placed Twila Hoffman's name, along with many others, on a witness list. The defense was allowed to see this list, and Berger learned later that Miranda's lawyer had left several messages for Hoffman, but that she had returned none of the calls. Flynn may have believed that Hoffman was just another name on this long list, rather than the prosecution's key witness.

Berger went to Hoffman's home with Officer Cooley and another police officer. She said, "Come on in." That was their first shock. Berger had thought that Hoffman would be uncooperative. Quite to the contrary, Hoffman was glad to talk about the case.

Hoffman told Berger and Cooley that Miranda had confessed the crime to her while he was in jail. He had told her that he had tied the victim up, taken her to the desert, and raped her.

After a long discussion with Hoffman, Berger asked why she was being so cooperative. As it turned out, while Miranda was in prison, Hoffman and one of her daughters (not Miranda's child) had gone to visit him. After that visit, Berger stated, Hoffman had reason to believe that, if Miranda got out of prison, he would harm Hoffman's daughter.[16]

During the trial, Hoffman testified that not only had Miranda confessed the crime to her, but he had also told

These mug shots, taken of Ernesto Miranda after his second conviction in the Rebecca Ann Johnson rape/kidnap case, are on file at the Arizona State Archives in Phoenix, Arizona. The letters across Miranda's forehead were stamped on the mug shot as part of the record-keeping process.

her to show Rebecca Ann their infant child. Perhaps seeing the child would encourage Rebecca Ann to drop the charges, he believed.[17]

Throughout Hoffman's testimony and the trial in its entirety, many legal matters were taken up before the judge. He characterized the trial as a "nine-day game of constitutional chess." During the lengthy trial, jurors heard testimony for only one day. Lawyers spent the rest of the time arguing legal matters.[18] The jurors were not allowed to hear those legal arguments.

Even without the confession, the jury convicted Miranda on the strength of Twila Hoffman's testimony. Miranda was sentenced to twenty to thirty years in prison.

Miranda was sent to prison, where he was quite popular among the inmates as a result of the famous decision. He appealed, but his conviction was upheld by the Arizona Supreme Court, and then by the United States Supreme Court.

Miranda requested parole on four successive occasions, but it was denied each time. His notoriety might well have been his downfall in repeated bids for freedom.

Ultimately, in December of 1972, Miranda was released on a split vote by the parole board. For the next three years, he was in and out of prison on a variety of

YOU HAVE THE RIGHT TO REMAIN SILENT

ANYTHING YOU SAY CAN BE USED AGAINST YOU IN A COURT OF LAW

YOU HAVE THE RIGHT TO THE PRESENCE OF AN ATTORNEY TO ASSIST YOU PRIOR TO QUESTIONING, AND TO BE WITH YOU DURING QUESTIONING, IF YOU SO DESIRE.

IF YOU CANNOT AFFORD AN ATTORNEY YOU HAVE THE RIGHT TO HAVE AN ATTORNEY APPOINTED FOR YOU PRIOR TO QUESTIONING.

DO YOU UNDERSTAND THESE RIGHTS?

WILL YOU VOLUNTARILY ANSWER MY QUESTIONS?

This *Miranda* card, which bears Ernesto Miranda's autograph and the date of the famous Supreme Court decision, is from the personal collection of Peter Baird, one of Miranda's attorneys.

charges. He continued to practice his barber trade behind bars.

When Miranda was released in 1975, he was unable to obtain employment as a barber because the law would not allow a barber's license to be issued to a person with his criminal record. Miranda went to work for a tire company. In order to supplement his income, he sold autographed Miranda warning cards for $1.50 to $2.00.[19]

On January 31, 1976, Miranda sat at a table in a bar, gambling in a card game with two other men. "Three dollars!" one of them shouted after an argument broke out.

The barmaid took the cards, and the three men began to fight. Miranda's hands were bloody afterwards, and he went into the rest room to wash.

Before he returned, one of the men who had been involved in the fight passed a large hooked-end folding knife to the other man who had fought with Miranda. "Here, you finish it," he said, and left the bar.

When Miranda came out of the rest room, he scuffled with the man who held the knife. As Miranda tried to wrestle the knife away, the man stabbed him twice, once in the abdomen, once in the chest. Miranda fell to the floor near the pool table. At the age of thirty-five, Ernesto

Ernesto Miranda is killed; subject of landmark case

Ernesto Miranda

Ernesto Miranda, whose rape conviction was overturned by the U.S. Supreme Court in 1966 in a landmark decision, was stabbed to death Saturday night in Phoenix in a fight over a barroom card game.

Miranda, 34, was stabbed in the chest and abdomen, police said.

He was stabbed by one of two men he had beaten in a fistfight minutes earlier in the La Amapola Bar, 231 S. Second St., Patrolman Gordon Costa said.

The killer, believed to be an illegal Mexican immigrant, was being sought in the downtown area.

Minutes after the slaying, police went to the Nogales Bar, 21 S. Second St., and arrested a man suspected of handing the knife to the killer.

The man, Fernando Zamora Rodriguez, 23, who was staying at the Reyes Hotel, 205 E. Jefferson, gave police a statement and was booked into Maricopa County jail for investigation of murder, according to Costa said.

Miranda's death made headlines in the Febrary 1, 1976 edition of the *Arizona Republic*.

Arturo Miranda was pronounced dead in the emergency room at Good Samaritan Hospital in Phoenix.

When a suspect was arrested in Miranda's murder, the arresting officer pulled out a warning card and began, "You have the right to remain silent . . ."[20]

Years later, Phoenix citizens would be protected by another officer who carried a Miranda warning card—Ernesto Miranda's nephew.*[21]

---

* As Justice Jackson wisely observed in *Korematsu* v. *United States,* "If any fundamental assumption underlies our system, it is that guilt is personal and not inheritable."[22]

6

Where We Stand Today

The deep division among the Supreme Court Justices in the *Miranda* decision mirrored the difference of opinion, one that still exists across the United States. Though many Americans supported the decision, an almost panicky response came from *Miranda's* critics. A breakdown of law and order was predicted. Many believed that confessions would essentially stop altogether. It was said that the Supreme Court had "handcuffed police" while bending over backwards to safeguard the rights of the "criminal" and ignoring the rights of the victim and the need for society to keep the streets safe.

Not only were critics worried about the predicted drastic decline in confessions and convictions, but they were also concerned about the time and cost of administering the *Miranda* warning and providing an attorney appointed at taxpayer expense. Critics were ready with the attack.

A Senate judiciary subcommittee called the judge from the second *Miranda* trial to testify regarding the impact of the case on law enforcement in the United States. Senator Sam Ervin called for a constitutional amendment to destroy the effect of the *Miranda* ruling.

Justice John Marshall Harlan, in his dissent to the ruling, predicted "harmful consequences for the country at large." And Duane Nedrud, then Executive Director of the National District Attorneys' Association and one of the "friends of the court" who had filed an amicus curiae brief, made a dire prediction, "Fewer crimes will be solved, even fewer crimes will be prosecuted." In addition, almost as a contradiction, Nedrud believed that, ironically, Ernesto Miranda, with an IQ of 70-75, would not even have been able to understand his constitutional rights if the *Miranda* warning had been given to him.[1]

In a setting where this warning was most likely to help those suspects who were poorly educated and uninformed, Nedrud's statement pointed out a true paradox.

Moise Berger, a prosecutor in Miranda's retrial, does

The Supreme Court Justices who read documents, listened to oral arguments, and handed down the decision in Ernesto Miranda's case were standing from left to right, Byron White, William J. Brennan Jr., Potter Stewart, and Abe Fortas. Seated from left to right are: Tom C. Clark, Hugo Black, Chief Justice Earl Warren, William O. Douglas, and John Marshall Harlan II.

not believe that the *Miranda* ruling helped anyone's rights or liberties. He feels that it was neither good for law enforcement nor the accused. "A lot of people went back on the streets who shouldn't have," he said. And he stated that many cases were thrown out of court because the law was incorrectly applied.

As to protecting the accused, according to Berger, whether or not a suspect talks has little or nothing to do with whether the suspect is told of *Miranda* rights. Berger cites a particularly brutal case where a man murdered his entire family. Berger was called to the scene by police. He asked a psychiatrist to meet him there. Berger and the psychiatrist spent a great deal of time explaining the suspect's rights to him, giving even more information than is required under the *Miranda* ruling.

Still, the suspect waived his rights and confessed to the murders. When Berger asked the psychiatrist why the suspect had confessed, the psychiatrist replied that the suspect felt guilty about what he had done and wanted to "get it off his chest."[2]

With controversy on many fronts regarding the *Miranda* ruling, the United States Congress in 1976 enacted a law in an attempt to dilute the *Miranda* decision. The law stated that the failure to give the *Miranda* warning would be only a factor in considering whether a confession was admissible.[3] As a practical matter, this law has not had a great impact on state cases which center on *Miranda* warning problems.

Stephen Markman, a former assistant attorney general in charge of the United States Office of Legal Policy, was one of the *Miranda* ruling's harshest critics. According to him, many people had begun to stray from a belief that the "principal concern of the justice system should . . . be the determination of truth." Instead, Markman said, many people had begun to believe that the justice system should be primarily concerned with a "narrowly defined range" of pseudo civil liberties for defendants. Markman stated in 1987, "Our present difficulties stem from having allowed these . . . civil libertarians to stand our Constitution on its head, and their tragic legacy can only be overcome if we put the Constitution back on its feet."[4]

As late as 1986, the twenty-year anniversary of the *Miranda* ruling, then United States Attorney General Edwin Meese drew his own conclusions about the case; ". . . I think what *Miranda* did was invent new rights that had never existed before 1966, and I think that the balance of the rights of the respective parties in the criminal justice system was imbalanced then." Meese's conclusions, and earlier predictions by *Miranda* ruling critics, however, did not seem to coincide with the vast majority of research about the actual effect of the decision.[5]

Though many believed that the *Miranda* ruling would cause the criminal justice "sky to fall," this prophecy simply has not come to pass.

On "Nightline," a television news program, Mario Merola, Bronx County (New York) District Attorney, appeared along with then Attorney General Edwin Meese in 1986. Merola's comment was quite the opposite of Meese's. Merola said, "I think that overall that [sic] *Miranda* has not hurt us. We're putting more people away than ever. We have more work than ever. So for us to deal with just a few cases, and you're concerned about that, really I think that *Miranda* is overblown."

Merola believed that the ruling had made police more fair. "There were cases where the individual is beaten and brutalized . . . by policemen who were interrogating, and I think that's what *Miranda* has done. It has civilized the whole operation, the criminal justice system and has civilized the police."[6]

As soon as six months after the ruling, Justice Tom C. Clark, one of the dissenting justices in the *Miranda* opinion, said that the decision had not hindered law enforcement as he had expected it might when he wrote his dissenting opinion. After talking to law enforcement officials across the country, Clark discovered that confessions were being made more frequently than before *Miranda*.[7]

Former Chief Justice Warren Burger also stated the view that *Miranda* has not had a negative impact on law enforcement.[8]

And in 1976, United States Attorney General Griffin Bell was quoted as saying, "It [the *Miranda* ruling] protects our rights under the Fifth and Sixth Amendments, and I don't know of any better alternative. It is part of the American way of life now. Even the police don't want to do away with it. And I talked to quite a number of them [while at the Justice Department]."[9]

Though some studies found to the contrary, in 1968 the Institute of Criminal Law and Procedure at Georgetown University found that the percentage of suspects questioned after the *Miranda* ruling dropped only slightly, from 55 to 48 percent.[10]

The anticipated overall drastic decline in confessions following the *Miranda* decision simply never seemed to materialize. Eville Younger, Los Angeles County District Attorney, made a study shortly after the ruling in order to determine its impact on law enforcement. What he learned is surprising. Of approximately four thousand felony cases prosecuted in a three-week period within the study, confessions were "essential to a succesful prosecution in only a small percentage of criminal cases." Younger's conclusions are interesting. "The most significant things about our findings are that suspects will talk regardless of the warnings, and furthermore, it isn't so all-fired important whether they talk or not."[11]

So, what about the fear that the *Miranda* ruling would be responsible for putting scores of menacing criminals back on the streets? Studies seem to bear out the fact that no such change is taking place. In a 1987 article in the *American Bar Association Journal*, John Kaplan, a law school professor, concluded that suspects offer confessions just as easily with the *Miranda* warnings as without. He concluded that suspects simply feel more inclined to talk when the police are courteous and professional.[12]

Of note is the fact that the *Miranda* ruling made a law of what the FBI had been doing for two decades, informing suspects of their rights. So the type of warnings required by the *Miranda* ruling were certainly nothing new in law enforcement.

And is the *Miranda* case truly worth all the controversy? In July of 1988, a *Newsweek* article reported that fewer than 1 percent of criminal cases had been thrown out because of defective confessions. And of the 1 percent, only a fraction were voided because law enforcement failed to follow *Miranda* guidelines.[13]

Did the doomsday predictions about the burden and expense of administering the *Miranda* warnings come to pass? The burden is certainly not as it was first feared to be. Police officers need only carry a small card or piece of paper and read suspects their rights—certainly no great investment of time.

As for the expense, it was feared that *Miranda* would cause a flood of attorneys to be appointed at the interrogation stage, at taxpayer expense. Again, this fear has proven unfounded.

The *Miranda* ruling does not require that all suspects have an attorney present at the time of in-custody interrogation. Rather, the opinion states that suspects have the right to have a lawyer present. An overwhelming majority of suspects continue to give up, or waive, the right. It is important to note here that even if a suspect waives the right to an attorney, any confession given must still be voluntary. In other words, just because a lawyer is not present during questioning, the interrogating officers do not have the right to coerce a confession from a suspect.

What has happened in the courts since the June 1966 *Miranda* ruling? Have any cases served to overrule this decision?

Though Supreme Court decisions have chipped away at the spirit of the decision, none has served to totally destroy its impact. After many years, the *Miranda* ruling remains intact.

Perhaps one of the earliest and most notable cases to affect the *Miranda* ruling was the 1971 decision, *Harris* v. *New York*. This case did something no other case had done. It allowed the limited use of a defendant's confession in court, even though the defendant had not been given the *Miranda* warnings. This use, it is critical to point out, however, was limited to impeachment or contradiction at the time of trial.[14]

The impeachment use comes into play only if the defendant who has given a confession does decide to testify in a criminal case. If, while testifying, the defendant makes comments that contradict statements in the confession he had made earlier, the confession may be used for impeachment purposes. The prosecutor is then allowed to ask the defendant about the contradictory statements in the confession. In this way, the jury actually does have the opportunity to hear the statements made by the defendant in the confession. Impeachment can be a great help in cross-examination, as jurors are less likely to believe the testimony of a witness who has contradicted earlier personal statements.

Before the *Harris* ruling, if the defendant's confession was obtained without a *Miranda* warning, the confession could not be used for any purpose in court. This has changed since the *Harris* decision was handed down.

The *Harris* impeachment opinion met with great

controversy. Those who oppose the *Harris* ruling argue that a confession made without the required warning is "tainted," or bad for all purposes. Those who support the impeachment decision, however, are pleased to see that the Supreme Court has chipped away at the *Miranda* decision. These supporters believe it is only right that if the defendant chooses to take the stand and testify, prosecutors are not forced to sit by while the defendant contradicts prior statements made in a confession.

In the 1974 case of *Michigan* v. *Tucker*, police failed to give the complete *Miranda* warning to the suspect in custody. The suspect was not advised that an attorney would be provided if he could not afford one. Still, the court upheld the conviction, stating that the other warnings had been given. The *Miranda* warnings are "not themselves rights protected by the Constitution," the Court stated, but are ". . . standards" to "safeguard" or "provide practical reinforcement."[15]

The ruling in the *Tucker* case, however, has done little to alter the *Miranda* warnings and the confession cases across the country.

In the *Duckworth* v. *Eagan* ruling of 1989, the Supreme Court perhaps whittled away a bit more at the *Miranda* decision. In that case, police officers advised the suspect that they were not able to provide an attorney at the time of interrogation. Officers advised the suspect, however, that an attorney would be appointed if and when the suspect went to court.

Surprisingly, in this case, the United States Supreme Court upheld the defendant's conviction, stating that no specific form for the warnings had been set down by the Court. Further, the Court stated that police were not required to provide "on call" lawyers for suspects.[16]

In another case, *North Carolina* v. *Butler* in 1979, the United States Supreme Court decided that the waiver of rights under the *Miranda* warnings does not have to be in writing.[17] Perhaps the first question that comes to mind in this setting is: What's to keep some police officers from simply saying that rights were waived in cases where the *Miranda* warnings were never actually given at all? After all, if oral waivers are acceptable, why not simply testify that the *Miranda* rights had been waived orally?

Initially, it must be understood that many ethical police officers protect citizens across the country. These ethical officers would not engage in this type of activity. A further safeguard, however, is provided in the law. In order to appreciate this safeguard, it is important to examine what actually happens in court. Any time a witness testifies, credibility is an important issue. Jurors may believe all, some, or none of what a witness says. This policy encourages police officers to get a *Miranda* waiver in writing rather than face a court challenge later regarding whether a waiver was made orally.

Looking at the *Miranda* warnings and the possible waiver of *Miranda* rights, it is logical to wonder what actually happens in court when a defendant challenges the admissibility of a confession. In order to make such a challenge, the lawyers must discuss the fact that a confession exists. And generally, the defendant takes the stand to testify about how the confession was obtained and whether warnings were given. But what about the Fifth Amendment privilege against self-incrimination? If the defendant does not want to testify but does want to raise a legal issue regarding the confession, what keeps the jury from hearing what the defendant and the lawyers have to say?

The defendant is entitled to a hearing, discussion by lawyers and the judge, in consideration of a point of law, in front of the judge regarding the confession itself. This hearing, held outside the presence of a jury, is for the sole purpose of determining whether the confession is admissible. Thus, if a defendant wants to challenge the admissibility of the confession but does not want the jury to even know that a confession exists, the defendant may testify without the jury in the courtroom. If the judge rules that the confession is not admissible and the defendant chooses not to testify, the jury hears nothing about a confession at all.

Even with the United States Supreme Court modifications of the *Miranda* decision, the Court appears to have no intention of overruling its opinion. As late as 1993, in the case of *Withrow* v. *United States*, the Supreme Court showed its support of the *Miranda* ruling. In the *Withrow* case, Supreme Court Justices stated that *Miranda* rights take precedence over other types of rights.

How far does the *Miranda* ruling go? What about evidence other than the defendant's confession that might be brought into court?

Suppose a suspect is taken to the hospital and blood is drawn while the suspect is unconscious. What happens if, as a result of the blood test, the suspect is charged with driving while intoxicated or driving while under the influence of drugs? Can the prosecutor inform the jury that the defendant's blood test revealed intoxication? The blood test would indeed tend to show the defendant's guilt. Is there a privilege against self-incrimination in this setting under the *Miranda* ruling? Would the police and prosecutors need a *Miranda* waiver from the defendant in order to bring blood test results to the jury?

No, because the rights under the *Miranda* ruling do not extend to protection from physical evidence, such as a blood test. These rights extend only to statements made by the suspect.[18]

In deciding *Miranda*-type cases, the Supreme Court is precariously perched on a tightrope. The Court is flexible in its ability to apply the law to a variety of fact situations. This is well illustrated by the cases that have followed the *Miranda* ruling.

As Justices retire from the United States Supreme Court and the president appoints new Justices to fill the vacancies, the application of the *Miranda* ruling and other cases will most certainly be affected. The varying composition of the Supreme Court has a profound impact on the criminal justice system.

The initial outcry over the effect of the *Miranda* ruling has died down considerably, though some critics remain vocal. Balancing the rights of the defendant with the rights of society and the victim has never been an easy task. As a famous legal scholar once said, "It is better that ten guilty persons escape than one innocent suffer." [19] This is one of the cornerstones upon which the United States criminal justice system has been built.

Undoubtedly, it can be difficult to determine who has actually committed a crime. Perhaps all signs point to guilt; however, the suspect may truly be innocent. In the United States, the accused is presumed innocent unless proven guilty beyond a reasonable doubt. Throughout the ages, bizarre twists and turns in criminal cases have shocked the public. Just when assumptions have been made and guilt seems obvious, a piece of evidence may surprise everyone. The right to have a criminal case heard in court, in order that evidence may be introduced and weighed, is a fundamental right of all Americans.

And this right is exercised in courtrooms across the country every day. When *Miranda* warning questions come into play in these courtrooms, a criminal justice system steeped in years of tradition and legal precedent goes into action to uncover evidence and produce results.

The *Miranda* v. *Arizona* ruling was reconsidered by the United States Supreme Court in June 2000 in *Dickerson* v. *United States*. By a strong 7–2 majority, the Court upheld the *Miranda* warning given by police to criminal suspects.

The majority decision in *Dickerson*, written by Chief Justice William Rehnquist, was a sharp defeat for those who had hoped that the Court would push aside *Miranda* in favor of a largely ignored law passed by Congress in 1968 to lessen its effect.

It is likely that the *Miranda* ruling will continue in force for many years to come. Thus, when future suspects are taken into custody, among the first words from the arresting officer will be,

You have the right to remain silent.

You Be the Judge

1. You are the lawyer for a person who is accused of burglary. You learn that your client, the accused, was not told that she had the right to remain silent. She was, however, told that she had the right to an attorney and that if she could not afford an attorney, one would be appointed to represent her. Your client signed a confession in which she waived her right to have an attorney present. What is your argument to the court regarding this confession?

2. You are the lawyer for a person who is accused of assault. The accused's primary language is Spanish, and he speaks very little English. The police officers explain that when the accused was arrested, he was given his

Miranda warning, then asked if he understood the warning. He nodded his head in the affirmative and replied, "Yes." After the police took the accused into an interrogation room at the police station, they had difficulty understanding him and asked that an interpreter come to translate. The interpreter did not give the *Miranda* warning to the accused in Spanish. During the questioning, the accused admitted having participated in the commission of a crime. What arguments would you make as the accused's attorney? What do you think the attorney for the state would have to say? How do you think the judge would rule?

3. Some say that people like Ernesto Miranda who are not well educated do not understand the *Miranda* warnings when they are given. What, then, is the purpose of the warnings? Should a new Supreme Court ruling come down to discontinue the warnings? Why? Why not?

4. Some political commentators have stated that the controversy over the *Miranda* ruling is overblown. They believe that whether or not a suspect gives a confession is of relatively little importance. What are the arguments that support this position?

5. The year is 1965. You have been appointed by the court to represent an indigent defendant. She was taken from the scene of a murder to the police station for questioning. She did not have a lawyer of her own, and she was not told that she had the right to have an attorney present at the time of questioning. Your client, of her own free will, without coercion, gave a confession to the police. The confession described the crime in detail. When the case was tried in the state court, you tried to keep the jury from hearing the confession. The judge allowed the confession to be heard, and your client was convicted. You and your client appealed the case to the state Supreme Court, where the conviction was upheld. Now the case has been appealed to the United States Supreme Court. Will you base your argument on the Fifth Amendment or the Sixth Amendment? Why?

6. You represent a defendant who was properly given his *Miranda* warnings after arrest, before questioning. He waived those rights and began to give the police a statement. After several minutes, your client reconsidered. He said that he did not wish to continue his confession and that he would like to have a lawyer. The police officers immediately stopped the questioning and requested that an attorney be provided. While your client sat in the interrogation room waiting for a lawyer,

he began to feel uncomfortable and decided that he should "come clean" and give the details of the crime he had committed. Before the lawyer arrived, he blurted out details of the crime to the police. What is your position regarding your client's confession? Why?

7. Comments are often made in the media regarding the "technicalities" of the law. Was Ernesto Miranda's case decided on a technicality? Should the law be changed so that cases cannot be decided on technicalities? Why? Why not?

8. A defendant was convicted of murder and sentenced to death. The murder was particularly brutal and left the victim's family in a shambles, both emotionally and financially. The defendant's conviction was based primarily on a confession given by the defendant without *Miranda* warnings. Now the defendant's conviction has been reversed. The United States Supreme Court has ruled that the confession may not be used in a future trial. The prosecution has insufficient evidence to convict without the confession, so the defendant will go free. Has there been an abuse of justice? Is it wrong that the defendant will be free as the result of a failure to give the *Miranda* warnings? Does this case give enough reason for the Supreme Court to

reverse its ruling in the *Miranda* case? If so, how far should the Supreme Court go in removing rights from the accused?

9. You are in law school, and you are very enthusiastic about practicing criminal defense law when you graduate. You will be defending a variety of clients, some of them like Ernesto Miranda. Your clients may sometimes admit to you that they have committed the crimes with which they are charged. You are approached by your sister and grandmother, both of whom have been victims of violent crimes. They are horrified by your choice and cannot imagine how you could possibly consider a career in which you would be defending "those murderers, baby abusers, and rapists." They want to know how you could set criminals free to roam the streets and commit crimes again. What do you tell them?

10. Those who support the *Miranda* decision and the line of confession cases leading up to it state that stricter laws regarding confessions require that police officers work harder. Without confessions, these supporters contend, officers must get out and work to find leads and hard evidence. In the second Ernesto Miranda trial, the state of Arizona introduced evidence from Twila Hoffman. Without Hoffman's testimony, it is unlikely

that Miranda would have been convicted. At Miranda's first trial, there was no testimony from Hoffman. Indeed, officers and prosecutors did not even learn about the information Hoffman had to offer until weeks before the second trial. Does this fact support the position that some officers may not work as hard to get information about a case if they can get a confession from the suspect? Why? Why not?

11. The psychiatrists who examined Ernesto Miranda found that he was emotionally ill. Should this emotional illness be a legal excuse for committing a crime? Why? Why not? If such emotional illness were a legal excuse for committing a crime, how would this affect our criminal justice system and our society at large?

12. You are an attorney representing a publishing colleague of John Lilburne's. Your client is facing lengthy imprisonment because he refuses to answer questions about criminal charges against him. What is your argument on your client's behalf?

Chapter Notes

Chapter 1

1. Richard C. Cortner and Clifford M. Lytle, *Constitutional Law and Politics: Three Arizona Case Studies* (Tucson, AZ.: The University of Arizona Press, 1971), p. 9.

2. As reported in the departmental records of the Phoenix, Arizona Police Department.

3. Ibid., Also: Trial transcripts of Miranda's first trial, as included in Petitioner's brief to the United States Supreme Court, RG 267, National Archives., pp. 22-23, 34-35.

4. As reported in the departmental records of the Phoenix, Arizona Police Department.

5. Ibid.

6. Liva Baker, *Miranda: Crime, Law, and Politics* (New York: Atheneum, 1983), p. 12.

Chapter 2

1. *Brown* v. *Mississippi*, 297 U.S. 278 (1936). [This is a direct citation to the Supreme Court decision.]

2. Peter Baird, "Miranda Memories," *Litigation* (Winter 1990), p. 43. Also: Herbert M. Atherton ed., *1791-1991: The Bill of Rights and Beyond.* Undated. pp. 41-42.

3. Lisa Baker, *Miranda: Crime, Law and Politics* (New York: Atheneum, 1983), p. 67.

4. *Miranda* v. *Arizona*, 384 U.S. 436 (1966). [This is a direct citation to the Supreme Court decision.]

5. Kermit L. Hall, editor-in-chief, *The Oxford Companion to the Supreme Court of the United States* (New York: Oxford University Press: 1992), pp. 661-662. Also: *Powell* v. *Alabama*, 287 U.S. 45 (1932). [This is a direct citation to the Supreme Court decision.]

6. Hall, p. 96. Also: *Brown* v. *Mississippi*, 297 U.S. 278 (1936).

7. Hall, pp. 552-553. Also: Gary Chamberlain, "Crime, Confessions, and the Supreme Court," *America* (July 8, 1967), pp. 32-33.

8. Ibid.

9. Ibid., p. 33.

10. Hall, *The Oxford Companion to the Supreme Court of the United States*, pp. 338-339. Also: *Gideon* v. *Wainwright*, 372 U.S. 335 (1963). [This is a direct citation to the Supreme Court decision.]

11. *Argersinger* v. *Hamlin*, 407 U.S. 103 (1972). [This is a direct citation to the Supreme Court decision.]

12. Baker, p. 76.

13. Hall, *The Oxford Companion to the Supreme Court of the United States*, pp. 518-519. Also: *Malloy* v. *Hogan*, 378 U.S. 1 (1964) [This is a direct citation to the Supreme Court decision.]

14. Andrew David, *Famous Supreme Court Cases* (Minneapolis, MN.: Lerner Publications, 1980), pp. 76-78. Also: *Escobedo* v. *Illinois*, 378 U.S. 478 (1964). [This is a direct citation to the Supreme Court decision.]

15. Baker, pp. 26-28.

16. As reported in departmental reports of the Phoenix, Arizona Police Department. Also: Trial transcripts of Miranda's first trial, as included in Petitioner's brief to the United States Supreme Court, RG 267, National Archives.

Chapter 3

1. As reported in departmental records of the Phoenix, Arizona Police Department.

2. Resources for this section are as follows:

Reports from psychiatrists James A. Kilgore, Jr., and Leo Rubinow.

Peter Baird, "Miranda Memories," *Litigation* (Winter 1990), p. 43. Also: Herbert M. Atherton ed., *1791-1991: The Bill of Rights and Beyond.* Undated. pp. 9-12.

3. Ibid., p. 12.

4. As reported in the departmental reports of the Phoenix, Arizona Police Department.

5. Baker, pp. 9-12.

6. As reported in the departmental reports of the Phoenix, Arizona Police Department. Also: Trial transcripts of Miranda's first trial, as included in the Petitioner's brief to the United States Supreme Court, RG 267, National Archives., pp. 40-41.

7. Baird, p. 44.

8. As reported in the psychiatric reports of James M. Kilgore, Jr., and Leo Rubinow.

9. Trial transcripts of Miranda's first trial, as included in the Petitioner's brief to the United States Supreme Court, RG 267, National Archives., p. 55.

10. Ibid., p. 41.

11. Ibid., pp. 36-45. Also: Respondent's brief filed in the United States Supreme Court, RG 267, National Archives., p. 19.

12. Baker, p. 13.

13. Trial transcripts of Miranda's first trial, as included in Petitioner's brief to the United States Supreme Court, RG 267, National Archives., p. 41.

14. Baird, p. 45.

15. *Miranda* v. *Arizona*, 98 Ariz. 18 (1965).

16. Baker, pp. 62-63. Also: Peter Baird, "The Confessions of Ernesto Arturo Miranda," *Arizona Attorney* (October 1991), p. 22.

17. Cortner and Lytle, p. 22. Also: Baird, "Confessions," p. 23.

18. Baker, p. 83.

19. Petitioner's brief before the United States Supreme Court, RG 267, National Archives., p. 49.

Chapter 4

1. From notation on the prosecutor's copy of departmental reports of the Phoenix, Arizona Police Department.

2. Ibid.

3. Judgment and Sentence, RG 107 Maricopa County, SG 8 Superior Court. Phoenix, AZ: Arizona State Archives, Department of Library, Archives and Public Records.

4. Trial transcripts of Miranda's first trial as included in Petitioner's brief to the United States Supreme Court, RG 267, National Archives.

5. Lisa Baker, *Miranda: Crime, Law and Politics* (New York: Atheneum, 1983), p. 22.

6. Trial transcripts of Miranda's first trial as included in Petitioner's brief to the United States Supreme Court, RG 267, National Archives.

7. Ibid., pp. 62-67.

8. Cortner and Lytle, *Constitutional Law and Politics,* p. 19.

9. *Miranda* v. *Arizona,* 98 Ariz. 18 (1965).

10. Baird, "The Confessions of Ernesto Arturo Miranda," *Arizona Attorney* (October 1991) pp. 22-23.

11. Baker, p. 84.

12. Petitioner's brief before the United States Supreme Court, RG 267, National Archives. Also: Audiotapes of oral arguments in the United States Supreme Court, Records of the Supreme Court of the United States, RG 267.575 and RG 267.576, National Archives.

13. Petitioner's brief before the United States Supreme Court, RG 267, National Archives.

Chapter 5

1. Baird, "Miranda Memories," p. 45.

2. Baker, *Miranda,* pp. 60-61.

3. Ibid., p. 63.

4. Ibid., pp. 87-88.

5. Ibid., p. 110.

6. Audiotapes of Oral Arguments in the United States Supreme Court, Records of the Supreme Court of the United States.

7. *Miranda* v. *Arizona,* 384 U.S. 436 (1966).

8. Ibid.

9. Ibid.

10. Baird, "The Confessions of Ernesto Arturo Miranda," *Arizona Attorney* (October 1991) pp. 24-25.

11. Dissent to *Miranda* v. *Arizona,* 384 U.S. 436 (1966).

12. Baker, p. 191.

13. Ibid., p. 192. Also: "Rapist Asked, 'Pray for Me,' Jury Is Told," *Arizona Republic,* 17 Feb. 1967.

14. "Jury Picked for Retrial of Miranda," *Arizona Republic,* 16 Feb. 1967.

15. Baker, p. 192.

16. Moise Berger, telephone conversation with author, July 30, 1993.

17. Trial transcripts, Ernesto Miranda retrial, RG 107 Maricopa County, SG 8 Superior Court. Phoenix, AZ: Arizona State Archives, Department of Library, Archives, and Public Records.

18. "Second Rape Conviction for Miranda," *Arizona Republic,* 25 Feb. 1967.

19. Baird, "Confessions," p. 25.

20. As reported in the departmental reports of the Phoenix, Arizona Police Department.

21. Baker, p. 385. Also: Phoenix Arizona Police Department Information Desk Personnel, conversation with author, July 5, 1993.

22. *Korematsu* v. *U.S.,* 323 U.S. 214 (1944).

Chapter 6

1. Gary Chamberlain, "Crime, Confessions and the Supreme Court," pp. 32-33.

2. Moise Berger, telephone conversation with author, July 30, 1993.

3. Discussion of U.S.C. 3501, in Ronald Colins, Thomas S. Schrock, and Robert C. Welsh, "Interrogational Rights: Reflections on *Miranda* v. *Arizona,*" 52 Southern California Law Review 1 (1978).

4. Jonathon I. Z. Agronsky, "Meese v. Miranda : The Final Countdown," *American Bar Association Journal* (November 1, 1987), p. 87.

5. "Miranda Ruling," "ABC Nightline," June 13, 1986.

6. Ibid.

7. Chamberlain, p. 33. Also: Tom C. Clark, "Gideon Revisited," 15 *Arizona Law Review* 343 (1973).

8. Peter Baird, "Critics Must Confess, *Miranda* was the Right Decision," *The Wall Street Journal,* June 13, 1991.

9. Agronsky, pp. 88-89.

10. "Miranda Decision Study Shows Weakness in Enforcement," *Arizona Republic,* May 14, 1986.

11. Chamberlain, p. 34.

12. Agronsky, pp. 88-89.

13. Baird, "Critics Must Confess." Also: "Fighting Crime by the Rules," *Newsweek* (July 18, 1988), p. 53.

14. *Harris* v. *New York,* 401 U.S. 221 (1971).

15. *Michigan* v. *Tucker,* 417 U.S. 433 (1974).

16. *Duckworth* v. *Eagan,* 492 U.S. 195 (1989).

17. *North Carolina* v. *Butler,* 441 U.S. 369 (1979).

18. *Schmerber* v. *California,* 384 U.S. 757 (1966).

19. Blackstone, Sir William, Commentaries [1765-1769], Introduction to Chapter 27.

Further Reading

Adams, Barbara Johnston. *Crime Mysteries*. New York: Franklin Watts, 1988.

Atherton, Herbert M., ed. *1791-1991: The Bill of Rights and Beyond*. U.S. Commission on the Bicentennial of the United States Constitution. Undated.

Barnes, Richard. *Graystone College*. Minneapolis, MN: Lerner, 1973.

Bernstein, Richard B., and Jerome Agel. *Into the Third Century: The Supreme Court*. New York: Walker, 1989.

David, Andrew. *Famous Supreme Court Cases*. Minneapolis, MN: Lerner, 1980.

Green, Carl, and William R. Sanford. *American Government: The Judiciary*. Vero Beach, FL: Rourke, 1990.

Habenstreit, Barbara. *Changing America and the Supreme Court*. New York: Julian Messner, 1970.

Harris, Richard. *Freedom Spent*. Boston: Little Brown, 1976.

Haskins, James. *The Scottsboro Boys*. New York: Holt, 1993.

Jenkins, George H. *American Government: The Constitution*. Vero Beach, FL: Rourke, 1990.

Landau, Elaine. *Teenage Violence*. Englewood Cliffs, NJ: Julian Messner, 1990.

Lewis, Anthony. *Gideon's Trumpet*. New York: Random House, 1964.

Lowe, William. *Human Rights: Blessings of Liberty: Safeguarding Civil Rights*. Vero Beach, FL: Rourke, 1992.

Monk, Richard C., ed. *Taking Sides: Clashing Views on*

Controversial Issues in Crime and Criminology. 2nd ed. Guilford, CT: Dushkin, 1991.

Ritchie, Donald A. *Know Your Government: The U.S. Constitution.* New York: Chelsea House, 1989.

Sexton, John, and Nat Brandt. *How Free Are We? What the Constitution Says We Can and Cannot Do.* New York: M. Evans, 1986.

Slate, John, and R. U. Steinberg. *Lawmen, Crimebusters, and Champions of Justice.* New York: Mallard, 1991.

Glossary

admissibility—Whether or not information about a case will be allowed to be heard in court. The judge rules on the admissibility of the evidence.

amicus curiae brief—A brief filed by someone who is not a party to the case, but who has an interest in the law that will be made as a result of the decision. "Amicus curiae" is a Latin term meaning "friend of the court."

appellant—The party who appeals a court decision to a higher court.

brief—A document filed by lawyers in support of an issue, or issues, of law.

burden of proof—The test that the prosecutor or plaintiff must meet in order to win the case. In a criminal case, the burden, beyond a reasonable doubt, is much more difficult to meet than the burden in a civil case, by a preponderance of the evidence.

case or controversy—A legal concept providing that Justices, and other federal judges, may rule only if an actual dispute is brought before them. Though Justices have the power to make law, they cannot make law regarding an issue that is not involved in a case that they are reviewing.

complaining witness—The victim in a criminal case.

credibility—The believability of, or weight to be given to, a witness's testimony. The jurors (or judge when there is no jury) may believe all, some, or none of what a witness has to say. This belief is based upon the witness's credibility.

defendant's failure to testify—In a criminal case, the defendant is under no legal obligation to testify. If the defendant chooses not to testify, the judge and the jury are not permitted to consider this failure to testify for any purpose.

defense attorney—The lawyer who represents the accused in a criminal case.

dissent—A disagreeing opinion to a court ruling. The written court ruling becomes law. The dissent does not.

due process—A legal concept consisting of many legal guarantees and providing that a person accused of a crime will be treated fairly. Due process is a safeguard against cruel or arbitrary procedures.

evidence—Information brought into court regarding a case. Evidence may consist of testimony, documents, and physical evidence, such as guns, knives, and other objects that are important to the case.

fruit of the poisonous tree—A legal concept providing that if evidence has been obtained illegally, it may not be used in court.

grounds—The legal reason for a lawyer's objection.

hearing—A discussion by the judge and lawyers regarding a matter of law. The jury is not allowed to hear the discussion.

impeachment—The process by which a witness's testimony is attacked. The witness may generally be discredited through prior inconsistent statements.

incorporation doctrine—The method through which the United States Supreme Court has held that most of the amendments in the Bill of Rights are applied to the states through the Fourteenth Amendment.

indigent—A defendant who is unable to pay for legal representation.

interrogation—The questioning of a witness or suspect by law enforcement officers.

judgment and sentence—The document filled out by court personnel after a guilty verdict and sentence have been handed down against a defendant in court. This document generally becomes public record.

lineup—The placing of a suspect with a group of people who are viewed by the victim or another witness to a crime. A lineup is supposed to include people of similar appearance. Generally, the suspect cannot see the victim/witness viewing the lineup. The lineup is sometimes called a "show-up".

majority opinion—The decision agreed upon by the majority of the Justices. The majority opinion is written and becomes law.

oral argument—The arguments made in person by parties to a case, and others with a legitimate interest in the case, before members of the court. Lawyers usually make a statement first, and then respond to questions asked by Justices.

pauper's form—This document must be filed with a petition for writ of certiorari if the defendant is indigent (unable to pay required fees for an appeal to the United States Supreme Court.)

petition for writ of certiorari—This document must be filed in order to request that the United States Supreme Court hear a case.

precedent—This term refers to a case, or to the body of law made up of prior decisions, on the same or similar legal questions.

prosecutor—An official, also known as a district attorney, who represents the state in criminal proceedings.

pro bono—A lawyer's acceptance of a case without charging a fee.

statute—A law.

testimony—The information given in court by witnesses in response to questions.

voir dire—The process by which prospective jurors are questioned and chosen. The term "voir dire" comes from a French phrase meaning "to tell the truth."

Index